Followers of Jesus

A Textbook for Juniors in Vacation Church Schools

ELIZABETH SCOTT WHITEHOUSE

Published for

The Interdenominational Committee on Co-operative
Publication of Vacation Church School Curriculum

By

THE WESTMINSTER PRESS
PHILADELPHIA

Copyright, 1942

THE WESTMINSTER PRESS

Printed in the United States of America

All rights reserved — no part of this book may be reproduced in any form without permission in writing from the publisher, except by a reviewer who wishes to quote brief passages in connection with a review in magazine or newspaper.

This text is prepared from a descriptive outline approved and copyrighted by the International Council of Religious Education and used by permission.

A Personal Message to Leaders

YOU are thinking of leading a group of Junior boys and girls this summer as they discover what it means to be followers of Jesus. You are hoping that your boys and girls will come to a new knowledge of the greatest of all leaders, and be won to his cause to whatever extent they can understand and make it their own. It is with the thought of helping in the realization of this purpose that this course has been written.

As you use this book, keep in mind that the plan it offers is only one of many possible ones for the realization of your purpose. No book can do a leader's thinking for him; all leaders must do their own thinking and planning. The suggestions contained in this book will help you most as they stimulate your own thinking in the special locality in which you will work. The author knows many boys and girls; she does not know the particular group you will be working with, nor their special needs and opportunities. You must plan with these in mind. Read carefully " Planning for Your Own Vacation School," beginning on page 13, and " General Plans for Conducting the Department," beginning on page 165. Note that Sessions 6 and 8 in Unit II, " Each in His Own Way," provide an opportunity for a specific missionary emphasis. Write early to your missionary headquarters for information if you intend to use a denominational emphasis.

This book goes forth with the earnest hope that you and your Juniors, as seekers together, will find joy and profit in the living and planning and working that will go on in your school. It goes forth with the prayer that this course will help leaders to make possible the kind of school where boys and girls will live and work together according to the teaching of Him who said, " Come, follow me."

Sincerely your friend,
Elizabeth S. Whitehouse

CONTENTS

	PAGE
Planning for Your Own Vacation School	13

Unit I. "Ye Are My Friends"

SESSIONS

1.	This Is Our School	17
2.	Who Can Be a Follower?	29
3.	Followers Serve in Many Ways	37
4.	Growing as Followers	44
5.	Looking Back and Thinking Ahead	47
6.	"Ye Are My Friends"	52
7.	Steadfast in Danger	56
8.	Steadfast in Difficulty	59
9.	When It Is Hard to Choose	63
10.	Growing Dependable	66

Unit II. Each in His Own Way

1.	What Can a Good Follower Do?	71
2.	Good Followers Have Given Us Our Bible	81
3.	Songs That Have Helped Us	85
4.	Pictures That Make Us Think	89
5.	Followers of Jesus	94
6.	Followers Who Worked for Peace	96
7.	Followers in Strange Places	102
8.	Good Followers Are Not Easily Discouraged	105
9.	We Too May Serve	108
10.	Each in His Own Way	110

The Story Section	113
General Plans for Conducting the Department	165

Planning for Your Own Vacation School

THINKING ABOUT PURPOSES

The Vacation Church School for Juniors should provide those experiences in Christian living which make for growth in Christian character. Opportunities for these experiences will come as Juniors purpose, plan, and work together, as they play and worship together in our school. Growth will take place as the Juniors increasingly understand the Christian principles which contribute to such living, as they become increasingly able to judge their own attitudes and achievements in the light of those principles, and as they make significant Christian choices themselves. The two units of this course will provide for boys and girls:

Opportunities for knowing something about the lives of great men in the Christian Church.

Opportunities to see what it meant and still means to people to know Jesus and the spirit of Jesus.

Joy in finding effective ways of working with God's purposes as they come increasingly to know them.

Awareness of the importance of individual contributions in making life happier and better.

Satisfaction in feeling themselves a part of a great plan, begun with the Early Church, which is still vitally alive in the world today.

Experience in discovering specific ways in which they themselves can carry on the work started by great Christian leaders of the past.

Each leader and teacher will want to read the two units provided in this course and will want to work out her own purposes in the work which she will be doing with boys and girls. She will also want to be ready to guide boys and girls in doing some worth-while purposing of their own.

HOW LONG IS THE SCHOOL TERM TO BE?

This course is planned for a school term of four weeks, but this time limit need not be rigidly followed. Many schools plan for a two-week term, while others have three- or four-week terms in mind. Here are some ways in which the course might be shortened or lengthened according to need:

Schools planned for two weeks may use either of the two ten-session units contained in this book. Both units are complete and self-contained; that is, neither depends on the other either to provide a background of understanding or for completion.

Schools planned for three weeks may use the first unit and either the first or the second week of the second unit. Or, the school may begin with a study of the followers of Jesus in the Early Church, which is the content for week 6 of Unit I, "'Ye Are My Friends,'" and continue consecutively with the whole of Unit II, "Each in His Own Way." The latter plan offers less difficulty in following through on the suggestions for pupil activities.

Schools planned for five weeks will find that units can be expanded in a variety of ways. For example, the first unit might continue a study of the activities of the Early Church by introducing some of the adventures of Paul the missionary. Or, they might think about their own church, finding out how it is like the Early Church in purpose and work, how that work is done, and what is the responsibility of each church member in the plans and work of his church.

Another possibility for expansion lies within the second unit, which might add studies of many another who, "each in his own way," has shown himself to be a follower of Jesus. Or week 10 might become the beginning of an additional week's work in which a study can be made of other well-known Christians who today are helping to make real what Christ meant when he spoke of the Kingdom of God.

There is still a third possibility for expansion by planning additional sessions which will develop further any study or activity under way. Related studies could be thus introduced. For example, Sessions 2, 3, 4, 5, of Unit II, "Each in His Own Way," offer rich opportunities to consider many who serve in these ways:

PLANNING FOR YOUR OWN VACATION SCHOOL

Giotto, Hofmann, as well as Fra Angelico; Tyndale as well as Wycliffe, or the Bible colporteurs and missionaries today who are bringing the Bible to many peoples in the language they understand. Stories of hymns and hymn writers might enrich still further whatever is done in Session 3. Any plan must include the contribution boys and girls are making and can make as followers of Jesus.

PLANNING FOR WORK MATERIALS

On page 177 there is a list of basic supplies which Vacation Church Schools are likely to need. This is followed by an additional list which shows how the activities chosen will govern what needs to be bought. Go over the basic list carefully; your school may have paste, pencils, crayons, or other items, though perhaps not enough for all departments of the school. There need not be enough scissors to go around — many of the opportunities for Christian living in your school will grow out of the need to share — but essential materials should be on hand in sufficient quantity before the first school session opens.

Check with each assistant at the close of the first session to make sure that you know exactly what activities are under way, and what additional supplies are needed. Decide which of these the school must provide and which you can expect your boys and girls to contribute. For example, if one group has chosen to dress dolls for a hospital following a visit there (though this will scarcely be a plan made the first day of school), needles, thimbles, scraps of cloth, perhaps the dolls themselves, can be brought from home. On the other hand, if a group is going to attempt to make slides, or a stained-glass window, or scenery for a play, the supplies needed will undoubtedly come out of the school fund; the additional lists and directions for making the activity need to be consulted before getting supplies. In schools where Juniors truly share the responsibility for all that is done, it is impossible to determine beforehand exactly what activities are likely to be chosen or what supplies will be needed. Therefore, be sure that some of the fund for working materials is kept back so that the later progress of the school will not be retarded, nor its work determined by what is on the closet shelves instead of by what is in the minds of boys and girls. The Juniors will profit by the need to plan carefully and in the light of available cash.

IF ENRICHMENT BOOKS ARE POSSIBLE

On page 180 there is a list of books related to the work of the school. No school would want to buy them all. Many schools already own a number of the books. Some schools have no money for the purchase of any books for leaders other than the course book itself. In some schools there is a little money that can be used for the purchase of three or four books which would offer valuable enrichment materials for the use of both pupils and teachers. The following list is suggested for those who have a little money for such additional source materials. The list assumes that Bibles and hymnals will be available in the Church School, and that a Bible dictionary can be borrowed from the minister or other friend of the school:

The Bible: A New Translation, by James Moffatt. Harper & Brothers. Price, $3.50 and up.

The Story of Our Bible, by Harold Hunting. Charles Scribner's Sons. Price, $2.50.

Far Round the World, by Grace W. McGavran. Friendship Press. Price: cloth, $1.00; paper, 50 cents.

Each with His Own Brush, by Daniel Johnson Fleming. Friendship Press. Price, $1.50.

As many of the pictures as funds permit, selected from the list on page 183. The selection should represent various artists, various periods of time, and various countries.

If the first unit only is to be taught, *The Story of Our Bible,* by Harold Hunting, and *Each with His Own Brush,* by Daniel Johnson Fleming, could be dropped from the list of essentials.

If you are teaching for the first time, it would be very helpful to read *Teaching Junior Boys and Girls,* by Mildred Moody Eakin. Abington-Cokesbury Press. Price, $1.25.

If you have no assistant to help to plan games, you may need such a book as *The Cokesbury Game Book,* by Arthur M. Depew. Abingdon-Cokesbury Press. Price, $1.75.

Unit I. "Ye Are My Friends"

SESSION 1. THIS IS OUR SCHOOL

THE TEACHER GETS READY

Read carefully "Planning for Your Own Vacation School" (found on pages 13–16) and "General Plans for Conducting the Department" (pages 165–197).

Read widely into the unit as a whole; note the suggested materials listed; they are part of your tools for teaching.

Be sure that you are familiar with the procedure for enrolling pupils. Your school may have adopted a different plan from the one suggested in this text.

Have ready the pictures (see page 183) and books, or the picture projector with slides or film, for use as the Juniors arrive. Plan how you will guide the Juniors in understanding and appreciating these.

If your school has little shelf or closet space, the Juniors will probably need some orange crates obtained from your grocer. The Juniors should be given opportunity to discover their needs and to plan at once for any necessary bookcases, supply shelves, work lockers, and so forth. Have some sandpaper ready for smoothing rough edges, but don't buy the paint yet. Let the Juniors decide the colors to be used.

Be sure that there are paper, pencils, paste, scissors, crayons, and water colors or poster paints ready for use. These are basic materials. Follow directions for mixing and using.

Prepare enough copies of the simple fact test on page 28 so that each Junior can have one. Leave plenty of space for the Juniors to check the right answers.

Be sure that there are enough Bibles available for use by the Juniors today and throughout the course. Copy on the board the references that will be used (see page 22).

Make yourself familiar with the story to be told. If you doubt your ability to tell a story, practice reading it aloud until you can do it well. A well-read story is always better than a poorly told one.

Plan carefully for the worship service. Be sure that suitable materials are at hand which a worship committee may use in planning a worship center: a vase of flowers, an attractive table cover or two, candles and candlesticks, pictures, a well-illustrated Bible with large print, thumbtacks or clips for hanging a picture, matches (kept in your purse until wanted) for lighting candles, other materials that allow for choice and variety in arrangement.

Read the section "Using Junior Committees" (page 171). Choosing committees is an important part of the plan for today.

Do not be confused by references to "assistants" if your school is so small that these are not necessary. It is quite possible for teachers of small Junior groups to carry full responsibility for leadership. Larger schools will need assistant teachers as suggested.

As you read the procedures which follow, keep in mind that these are only suggestions. Some courageous planning on your own part is worth fifty finished plans which a teacher accepts without thinking them through in terms of her own purposes, her own pupils and their needs, and her own school and equipment. Feel free to make plans with your own Juniors from day to day in the light of all that has gone before.

A SUGGESTED PROCEDURE

Welcoming Juniors	Discussion of Bible reading
Examination of materials and informal planning	A game
	Group planning
Taking a test	Recess
Questions and reports	Committee and group work
Telling a story	Preparation for worship
Bible study	Worship service

As the Juniors Arrive. Greet each Junior as he arrives; try to fix first names in mind. Introducing Juniors to one another will help; asking for helpers to get the room ready for work, and calling each by name as he responds will aid you in learning names. See that each Junior either has been enrolled before coming into the room, or is enrolled immediately after arriving. It is important to begin with records as accurate and as complete as possible.

Examination of Materials. Call attention to the pictures you have displayed on the bulletin board or table; invite the Juniors to examine these. If you have been able to secure any of the books listed for Junior use (see page 180), these should be ready. The teacher, or the assistant, might motivate this first examination with a statement such as: " Later we are going to talk over any new discoveries you make about Jesus and his followers. If you find a story or a picture that puzzles you, don't be afraid to ask questions. Be sure that you can find the book or picture again, for you will be invited to bring it into conference with you later."

If the group is one that is largely without Sunday School experience, this first examination of books and pictures will need to be carefully guided. A possible approach would be: " Do you know what a leader is? Do you know what a follower is? There are some books and pictures here that tell us something about some followers and their Leader. See if you can tell who the Leader is, and some things he did. See if you can find a picture or story which tells one thing that this Leader did. See if you can find something about this Leader that you did not know before. Don't forget what you discover. We shall want to hear about it."

Planning for Care and Use of Materials. After a brief examination has been made, suggest that the Juniors think of some way to arrange these materials so that they can be cared for and used conveniently. If the department lacks sufficient shelf or closet space, invite the Juniors to make suggestions. Call attention to the orange crates or boxes that you have provided. Guide the Juniors in an investigation of possible ways of using them and of placing them. If there is time, preliminary work on sandpapering edges can be started. If the department does not need such temporary furniture, let the Juniors plan places for the safekeeping of all working materials on hand in the space available. Let them try out their ideas. They may test their plans by the following: " Is this a safe place in which to keep these materials? Will they be free from dust and from the wear and tear of unnecessary handling? Are these places convenient for those who must find and use these materials? " This is the time to appoint two or three Juniors to act as a supplies committee for the first week of school. Let the group discuss the duties of the committee. (You have already read committee duties on page 171.)

If You Have a Projector. If the school has a stereopticon machine or a film-strip projector, invite the group to gather in a convenient place for a ten-minute period of looking at projected pictures (see pages 184, 185 for picture suggestions).

Taking a Test. When all Juniors are registered and present, ask each of them to take a pencil and a copy of the test which you have ready on your desk for distribution. Invite them to make themselves comfortable somewhere in the room where they can think and work quietly. Explain that the test is to help us to discover what the whole group already knows about Jesus and his followers, so that we shall not waste time in our work. At the end of five minutes ask each Junior to write his name in the upper right corner, and collect the papers. These tests will not be discussed today, but will be most useful as you plan further for this unit (see the next session).

Getting Acquainted. Invite the Juniors into the circle for a conference period, explaining that we need time to know one another by name and time to make plans for our school. Ask the group to suggest a plan that will help us to know one another by name. Perhaps some Junior will suggest that each one before speaking might tell his name or write it on the board. Write your own name on the board. Suggest that we try to remember names so that we shall soon feel that we are working with friends we know.

For Discussion. "There are many people who share this world with us. Most of them have a plan for living. Some people's plans call for getting all that they can for themselves; some plans include ways of getting along with others. If you were asked to make a plan which would really help to make this the best possible sort of world, what would you put in your plan? Can you tell where you got any of the ideas for your plan?"

Perhaps the Juniors will be conscious of getting some of their ideas at home, at church, at school. Do not prolong this part of the discussion; accept their responses and comment that it might be interesting to think more about that. If they suggest that some ideas came from the materials examined this morning, ask them to tell about their discoveries. Otherwise you might continue:

"Once there was a Leader who lived by a plan. He said it was God's plan whereby all his children on earth might live happily together. Do you know what Leader I am thinking of? Do you think it might be worth while to think about his plan and try it out? Perhaps in our school this summer we can really experiment with some plans for living together as followers of Jesus our Leader. As you looked at books and pictures this morning, perhaps you discovered something about the kind of work done by Jesus and his followers. This might help us to know more about his plan. Tell us about your discoveries."

Let the Juniors bring to the group the book or picture that they are talking about. If books and pictures are not available, the Juniors may suggest instead something each would like the group to help him to find out about Jesus, his followers, and his plan for living. Such questions as the following will set the stage for further thinking (do not use them all):

Are there other things you would like to know about Jesus and his followers?

Do you know any of his followers by name? how they earned their living?

How do you suppose Jesus worked with his friends? Do you think that he always told them exactly what they were to do? How might they themselves have discovered ways of helping?

If people today would really learn and use Jesus' plan for living together in our world, how might the world be different?

Do you think that Jesus needs helpers to make the plan work? Name some.

Write these questions on the board or on a large sheet of smooth wrapping paper tacked on the wall. Keep a record of the Juniors' answers as they dictate them after discussion. Propose that the Juniors erase or cross out questions already answered. As work progresses, anyone should feel free to add new questions that occur in the work together.

Summing Up. "What is it we are trying to do in our school? [Make a plan for living which we can really use; discover the plan that Jesus used and taught for any help that it can give us in our plan-making.] If we could find his plan, do you suppose that it would be an easy one to live by? Why do you think it might be a plan worth thinking about and trying out?"

A Story to Tell or Read. "Come, Follow Me" (see page 113).

Reading from the Bible About Jesus' Need for Helpers. Let the Juniors help themselves to Bibles from the table or desk. If the group is large, ask for two volunteers to pass them. See that each Junior knows how to find the books of Matthew, Mark, Luke, and John, about three quarters of the way along in the Bible. Explain that these four books were written by friends and followers of Jesus. Ask the Juniors to turn to the beginning of one of the books (they need not all find the same book for this) and read the title. Explain, if no one knows, that gospel means "good news," and that each of the four stories of Jesus is called "good news." Ask if they can think why.

Call attention to the Bible references which you have copied on the board. Ask the group to notice how the references are divided into two groups. Call on someone to read the question which heads the first group of references. Call for volunteers to choose one of these for reading. More than one reader may work on a reference if the group is a large one. Remind them that they should read to find an answer to the question asked. Repeat the same procedure in the distribution of the other group of references. If some Juniors do not know how to find chapter and verse, ask each Junior who does know how to locate references to help one other Junior to find his reference. Check to see that all Juniors can read a reference; that is, that they know that a dash between verses (as, 4–8) means to read verses 4, 5, 6, 7, 8.

What Were Some of Jesus' Plans for Worthy Living?		How Did His Friends Help Him?
Matthew 5:23–25a	Luke 6:35a	Matthew 10:1, 5, 7, 8
Matthew 28:19, 20	Luke 6:38	Matthew 14:13–20
Luke 6:27, 28	John 14:15	Luke 22:7–13
Luke 6:31	John 15:12–17	John 4:4–8
		John 12:20–22

Allow at least five minutes for finding and reading the passage chosen, and then call for reports on the reading. Each Junior should tell which group of readings he is reporting on, and how his reading helped him to answer the question asked. Encourage all to make their reports in their own words; reading a reference aloud does not require thought about what has been read. When all the readings have been reported suggest that the group think about the questions asked by you or by them before the story. Are there any that they can answer now which they could not answer then? Be sure to note whether or not any of the Juniors' own listed questions have been answered. Close the discussion by listing answers under both questions which were used to guide the Bible-reading. There should be some group agreement in these answers, so that they will represent the thinking of all.

Material to Memorize. The Juniors may choose one or more of the passages read today as their memory work for the week. Remind them that ability to agree after thinking about several of the best-liked passages shows that they have found one way of working together, that it is according to the plan Jesus came to tell us about, for it requires thinking of the wishes of others as well as our own. One possible passage is Matthew 28:19, 20, but let the Juniors choose if they will.

A Game. Suggest that the group take a ten-minute play period for some active game, and then all come together for a planning period. Some game suggestions are given on page 178.

Planning for Our School. Examination of materials, Bible reading, and discussion should have provided the Juniors with ideas for further investigations to be made either together or individually. They will want to know more of the followers of Jesus down through the years, more about what it means to be a follower today. There are many ways in which such investigations may be made. The Juniors may suggest such methods as reading and hearing stories, interviews with adult Christians in the community, looking at pictures, reading what Jesus' friends wrote in the Bible about Jesus' plan for worthy living and what it means to be a follower of his. Some of the things they will need to think about in connection with investigations are:

What resources do we have or can we get? [This may include lending Bible storybooks to one another, borrowing books from the library, and so forth.]

How can we use and care for borrowed materials (including care in using, fair play in taking turns, care in keeping such materials)?

How can we keep a record of the discoveries we make?

They will also need to think about their general plans for their school: "Do we need committees to help us? Let's think of our plans for today. What do they include?" (Work, play, study, worship, and so forth). Suggestions concerning Junior committees are made on page 171. These will help you to guide the Juniors in constructive planning. A supply committee has already been chosen and instructed. Questions to be considered are: "Who will see that our room is ready for work and worship? What ought a room committee to do? Shall we need a game committee to help us to plan games; to make suggestions that will help everyone to have a good time; to point out problems that we ought to solve or make some rules for? Are there things to be done before we are ready to worship in our school? Would a worship committee help us to have a better worship time? How? What could we do to help such a committee?" Such a discussion will again help the Juniors to see that living and working together as Christians means, not only knowing what we want, but knowing how to plan so that the group as a whole gets the most out of all that happens in our school. It is important to know Jesus' plan for living as he lived it himself and taught it to his disciples and their followers if we would discover how we can make living together in our world a really happy experience.

The planning period should not break up until needed committees are appointed and some plan of work is started, with responsibilities allocated to individuals, groups, or committees. For example, a group may volunteer to make orange-box bookcases for the care of books, smoothing, painting, and placing them advantageously for the convenience of all. One or two groups might plan some way of recording discoveries made about followers of Jesus through what they heard read today. Such a record might consist in making a book, beginning a series of posters, dramatizing some incident in the life of the disciples, or planning to represent them in a panel of a stained-glass window or on slides which when completed will tell us much about followers of Jesus both long ago and now (see page 186 ff. for directions for interesting ways of keeping such records).

The game committee might meet together to plan one or two games for use at recess. Planning includes knowing who will explain game rules or directions as well as what games will be played.

Recess. This should be a period of free play, though the new game committee should be ready with suggestions. An adult supervisor needs to be on hand, not to direct games or play, but just to see that everyone has an opportunity to play and that the period is running smoothly.

Group and Committee Work Period. Some part of this period today may be needed for further planning, perhaps, as work gets under way. Needed materials may be lacking and some plan for getting them must be arranged. If there are several groups, assistant teachers will be needed to guide discussion. Some group may not be sure of the best way to go about mixing paint or what sort of paper is needed for bookmaking or for designing a stained-glass window. Or, the Juniors may not know what are good steps in making slides or planning a play. Some time must be taken for any needed experimenting or planning with the teacher what supplies can be bought by the school and what brought from home by the Juniors themselves, but on the whole some actual work can be done today on any enterprise undertaken.

The new worship committee may withdraw quietly from the other workers a few minutes before preparation for worship is begun. They may see that the chairs are well arranged for worship, that hymnbooks are ready. A simple worship center will help the group to feel like worshiping. This may be only a picture of Christ hung against a dark curtain, with a bowl of field flowers beneath to add color and beauty. The committee will plan in the light of the resources you have made available.

It is important that no Junior group undertake too much, or too elaborate plans, until the members have had time to work together and to discover exactly what they have to work with. At this point a simple plan which can be easily worked out, and parts of which can be completed in one or two sessions, is desirable, so that the maximum time for planning and thinking through possibilities is allowed. The Juniors must understand from the beginning that while they are free to choose and plan, they are responsible for finishing what is undertaken, and for seeing that it has value and beauty when completed.

Preparation for Worship. Give the Juniors five minutes' notice before it is time to finish their work. A few soft chords or the playing of a quiet hymn may call the group together in the place prepared by the worship committee. Perhaps the pastor can come and talk a few moments to the group, explaining why we worship, what real worship is, and how worship helps the followers of Jesus who have chosen his plan for living together. Or you may select two or three hymns which tend to create a worshipful atmosphere and invite the Juniors to sing these and perhaps one or two favorite hymns of their own. Ask them to choose favorite hymns which make us think of Jesus our Leader and of ways in which we may work with him.

The Worship Service.

QUIET MUSIC. (Often good and easy-to-play selections are offered in the back of the Junior book of music used in the department.)

CALL TO WORSHIP (*led by a Junior member of the worship committee*):

"Let the peoples praise thee, O God;
Let all the peoples praise thee."

HYMN: "Tell Me the Stories of Jesus."

BIBLE READING: Something Jesus Said to His Followers (*read by a member of the worship committee*). John 15:9-14.

PRAYER (*offered by leader*): Our Father, bless our school and us who have come to learn of you. We want to know more of Jesus, whom you sent to be our Friend and Leader. We have set ourselves to find out what it means to be his followers, so that we may follow him and work with him in making this a better and happier world. Be with us as we go to our homes today, and bring us together again tomorrow ready for work and play. We ask this in the name of Jesus, whom we love. Amen.

OFFERING and RESPONSE.

SONG: "O Master of the Loving Heart" (or some other suitable familiar hymn).

CLOSING PRAYER (*unison*): Lord, teach us what it means to be your loyal followers, we pray. Amen.

IF THERE IS TO BE A WORKERS' CONFERENCE

Some things that may need attention today are the following:

Whether or not records of enrollment are completed.

How the department teacher can get hold of names and addresses of her Juniors: how she will make available hereafter the attendance record.

Which assistant will take this attendance record daily, and when and how?

What new working materials are indicated by Junior planning today?

How will these be purchased, and by whom?

Any special problem noted within the group, such as some child's difficulty in understanding English or finding Bible references, some tendency toward domineering on the part of some boy or girl.

How will these be handled? By whom?

The teacher and assistants will also want to make note of the strong points of the session, sum up the work accomplished, and make plans that will insure the smooth ongoing of work, beginning at the very point where it was left today. The teacher and assistants will want to look together at the next session plan in this connection, in order to see what adaptations will need to be made in the light of what was planned by the Juniors today.

Make a note of all the questions asked, or significant responses made by the Juniors today, even though these have been written on the board. Boards are often cleaned without thought of the permanent value of what is written there, and a permanent record will be needed.

Be sure that every assistant knows what are her responsibilities for tomorrow's session. The play supervisor and pianist will be interested in the special suggestions planned for them at the beginning of Session 2.

A TEST FOR JUNIORS

Here are seven questions for you to think about. Each question has three possible answers given. Read the question slowly, then read the three answers underneath. Put an X by the answer you think is the best answer.

1. How did Jesus help people?
    By advising people to get everything they wish by praying for it.
    By showing God's love for men, and explaining how to work with God.
    By offering his help so that no one need try to do anything for himself.
2. What kind of people did Jesus say might be his followers?
    His rich fellow countrymen.
    The poor people who lived in his own land.
    All people everywhere who wished to follow him.
3. What were Jesus' disciples like?
    They were always good.
    They always did what was wrong.
    They were sometimes good and sometimes wrong.
4. What did Jesus' followers do?
    They helped Jesus in his work for others.
    They earned much money for themselves.
    They gave everything away to others.
5. What kind of helpers does Jesus need today?
    Helpers who can get the best for themselves.
    Helpers who will see that all have a fair share.
    Helpers who never keep anything for themselves.
6. Who can be Jesus' follower today?
    Anyone who loves Jesus and tries to help others.
    Only people who are grown up.
    Children who never do anything wrong.
7. How can Jesus' followers today help him?
    By waiting until they can do big, important things for him.
    By doing whatever they can to make others happier.
    By helping only those who do things for them in return.

CORRECT ANSWERS TO THE TEST

1. Statement 2.
2. Statement 3.
3. Statement 3.
4. Statement 1.
5. Statement 2.
6. Statement 1.
7. Statement 2.

SESSION 2. WHO CAN BE A FOLLOWER?

THE TEACHER GETS READY

Read through the plan for today carefully. It is going to require some adaptation in the light of what happened in your department yesterday.

See that the play supervisor, the pianist, and other assistants know what is expected of them; each must be sure of your hearty co-operation with any plans they may make. The same is true of the Junior committees appointed and instructed yesterday. Share responsibilities with all helpers; don't try to do their thinking for them.

Note the suggestions for helping Juniors to evaluate their own work. Criticism should grow out of a genuine desire to help; never allow it to degenerate into faultfinding.

Review your notes made on the results of the test. Which questions were most commonly answered wrong? This test deals, not so much with facts, as with ideas as to what it means to be a Christian or follower of Jesus; hence its importance.

Plan to make the Bible study one of the most interesting parts of the morning session. As you call for the discussion of the questions proposed with the references, remember that there may be no one "right" answer, but that the Juniors should be encouraged to read with purpose, and to report personal findings and reactions. Guidance can best be given through skillful thought-provoking questions, rather than through making dogmatic statements for the Juniors to accept.

The Scripture references and questions to be used in Bible study should be on the board before school begins.

Prepare your story with care; it has a contribution to make in helping the Juniors to think things through.

Hold yourself ready at any time to consult with any inquiring assistant or Junior; do not interfere with group work while it is being directed by the assistant in charge.

Plan so that your work with the Junior committees will be most profitable to them. The room and supplies committees will probably be on hand early to help you to get both room and supplies ready for Junior working groups to use. Note that today a little more responsibility is left to the worship committee. Note, too, that the service still remains very simple and brief. Only one new procedure has been added. The game committee needs a time for meeting before recess.

A SUGGESTED PROCEDURE

Outdoor play
Evaluation of work under way
Work period
Discussion and study
Telling or reading a story
Recess
Work on record
Preparation for worship
The worship service
Workers' conference

On the Playground. The play supervisor should be on hand before the arrival of the first Junior. The supervisor should talk over plans for this early period with any member of the game committee who comes early enough for this. Call on the committee to choose games, explain the rules to the rest of the group, and help in seeing that all have an opportunity to play. Supervised play provides a genuine situation within which children may be guided to real growth in Christian attitudes and habits. Such attitudes are listed below and indicate why play is a basic part in the plan for the school:

Fair play (another term for honesty).
Obeying the rules of the game because those rules are understood and assented to.
Co-operating with comrades and leader.
Self-control which insures skill and makes for true leadership.
Good will and honest consideration of others.

Good sportsmanship, which means ability to win without boasting or to lose without anger or sulking.

Loyalty to the school or group, and to its aims and plans because the Juniors recognize them as their own in which all share equally.

The supervisor should not make decisions herself as to what is right and good, but should try to guide the Juniors in an honest criticism of playground happenings, as well as in planning and trying out remedies that make for better spirit and co-operation. "You chose the game yesterday, Tom; suppose you pick out a game chooser today," may be a tactful way of insuring turns for all without discouraging a potential leader. Arguments are best handled by trying to get a clear statement of the point of disagreement, then asking for the game rule involved, or calling upon the game committee or the group as a whole to suggest appropriate action. Practice in meeting situations means increasing recognition of the need for rules and obedience to those proposed or accepted by the group.

Entrance Into School. The room should be neat and orderly, with needed supplies conveniently arranged. This work will have been done in advance by the room and supplies committees.

If possible use music to call attention to the fact that the morning work period has arrived. Perhaps a piano can be moved close to the window for this. If that cannot be done, a Junior bugler might sound the call, or the supervisor of play might ask the game committee to work out some signal that could be used as a means of informing the playground of the time. Try to avoid using a bell, clapping, or shouts to secure attention.

Evaluation of Work Under Way. When any enterprise is just beginning, or when it is approaching completion, it is well to call for a review of purpose and plan, and for a critical evaluation of the work under way in the light of that purpose and plan. This will not be required every day, and should never take more than five or six minutes unless some major problem is to be faced. If orange-crate furniture is being made, the Juniors working on it may be called on for a report. Some Junior who has not helped with this might be asked to inspect the work. He can be stimulated by group suggestions as to what to look for: "Is there danger of splinters? Are the boxes clean inside where books and borrowed materials are to be kept? Is the paint a good color [if painting has begun or is planned for] — one that we shall enjoy living with? Are there enough bookcases being made to care for our needs (remembering that our need for space will grow as our school continues)?"

Likewise the records of discoveries begun yesterday should be explained in detail by groups working on these. Again plan and purpose should be emphasized, and the work evaluated in terms of these. Encourage the group to make thoughtful suggestions for improvement whenever they offer a criticism. See also that proper appreciation of what is good and useful is voiced by the group. Perhaps next steps will need to be planned by some of the groups at work.

This may be the time to plan gifts to be made for some special persons or group. Some Junior may recall that part of Jesus' plan for worthy living was thinking of others, and how to make them glad. Perhaps there is a near-by day nursery or children's hospital where cutout toys would be appreciated if made smoothly and attractively (see page 193 for suggestions). Or there may be younger children at home who would appreciate such gifts. Other suggestions of things to do may come from the group. Those not at work on some other enterprise may begin such construction immediately this morning. Encourage general willingness, however, to tarry with the main group while there are still major problems in connection with any group's work; this increases the feeling of responsibility for the department as a whole on the part of all. Any new agreements as to work or plans should be recorded on the board.

Work Period. If the Junior Department is large, the various working groups or committees should meet with the assistants in charge. The working groups will want to keep in mind any helpful suggestions or criticisms coming out of the earlier discussion. The game committee will need time to plan games, and to suggest rules if need for rules has arisen on the playground, as preparation for recess. The members of this committee might withdraw from the working groups long enough to do this planning.

WHO CAN BE A FOLLOWER?

Discussion and Study. After a warning chord on the piano, the group will put away work and gather for study and discussion. The following are questions that ought to start the group members thinking together:

"Did anyone discover something new about Jesus yesterday? about what it means to be a follower of his?

"What were some of the things we decided that we want to find out in our school?

"Have we found answers to any of the questions we listed yesterday?

"Who would you say can be a helper of Jesus? Must he be someone who is very wise? someone grown up? someone who is always good? Would you say that it must be someone who is very skillful at some art or trade? If you really want to know what sort of folks Jesus can use as helpers, where will you look for information?" (The group will probably suggest looking in the Bible to see what sort of people helped, on what Jesus said about helpers. Let the Juniors get their Bibles.)

The group members are still rather unused to thinking together, so that there may be little give-and-take today; nevertheless there should be some interchange of thought. Call on someone to express an opinion about something said; give opportunities to evaluate responses as given, to add to them, to express judgment as to their workability in the light of what has been planned for the school. Remember, this is a period for real thinking; work for free discussion in which each member of the group takes part. Keep in mind also that all discussion should be in the direction of a conclusion. This does not mean that the group members will reach a conclusion today, or that, granting they do, they will not change their conclusion tomorrow as thinking and growing continue. Definite thinking in connection with real problems and ideas promotes discussion, finds solutions to problems, and promotes growth in attitudes and ideas.

Discussing the Tests. Bring out the tests taken yesterday. Call attention to the number of questions most Juniors answered correctly. Comment on the fact that this shows something of what we already know about Jesus and his followers, and pull these facts together by reading the questions correctly answered and letting the Juniors answer them orally now. Use the Bibles to help the group to find the correct answers to questions most frequently missed. The following passages will help in understanding the correct statements under each question:

1. Matthew 4:23
2. Mark 3:35; John 8:31
3. Mark 10:28; Mark 9:33, 34
4. Matthew 14:14-20; Luke 9:1, 2
5. Romans 13:7, 8, 10
6. John 13:34, 35
7. Acts 10:38; III John 11

Bible Study for Information. " In our Bible reading today we shall hear of several kinds of people. When you find the word ' Samaritan ' in your reading, remember that the Samaritans were foreigners, especially hated by the Jews. When you read the word ' publican,' remember that a publican was a taxgatherer. The Jews did not like taxgatherers because they said, ' God is our king, and no one has a right to make us pay taxes to any other king.' Also, most taxgatherers forced the people to pay more than the king demanded.

" On the board I have written five Bible references. They are all found in the first four books of the New Testament which you located yesterday. Please notice that under each reference there are questions for you to think about as you read. We shall want to talk about these later."

Assign the following references to the Juniors, perhaps by dividing the group into five parts and assigning one of the references to each:

John 4:4-9, 27-30, 39-41

Could Jesus, a Jew, hope to be welcomed into a Samaritan city?
How did a Samaritan woman help Jesus?

Mark 1:16-20

Why do you think Jesus chose these fishermen for helpers?
What do you think Jesus would expect of them?

Luke 10:30-35

Why did two men fail as helpers to the injured man?
What made the Samaritan a better helper than the other two men?

WHO CAN BE A FOLLOWER?

Luke 17:11–19

What difference do you suppose it made to Jesus that one man came back to thank him?

Do you suppose the man ever did anything afterward that helped Jesus? What might he have done?

Luke 19:1–8

How did Zacchaeus help Jesus?

Which of the things he did do you think pleased Jesus most?

Allow time for reading and thinking, but do not allow the study period to drag. Call for reports and discussion of the questions.

Story. "Levi the Outcast Finds a New Friend" (see page 116).

Thinking It Through. "From what you have read and heard today, what would you say if someone asked you, 'Who can be a follower of Jesus?' How would you describe the sort of person who would make a good helper for Jesus?"

Memory Work. Continue with the passage chosen yesterday.

Recess. Play under the supervision of the assistant in charge. This does not mean that the assistant will plan all the games! The game committee is prepared to help at that point.

Working on Our Record. Use this period to work on enterprises chosen yesterday as a means of recording discoveries about Jesus' plan for worthy living, about followers, or about some other phase of the work under way. The assistants in charge of this should help the Juniors to keep in mind any helpful criticisms or suggestions made earlier in the morning.

The worship committee should be called upon to work out plans with the teacher during this period. In planning the worship center, they may use the plan worked out yesterday or they may change it entirely. Two lighted candles arranged on either side of an open Bible on an attractively covered table suggest that something beautiful and worth-while is about to happen. Enrichment and variety should be made possible by the teacher and assistants, keeping on hand suitable materials which will make a pleasant change in arrangement without losing the simplicity and dignity necessary for our worship purpose. Color schemes are easily changed by having a variety of table covers to choose from. Pictures can be chosen afresh from picture resources, fresh flowers brought from gardens or from roadsides.

Preparation for Worship. Recall the meaning and purpose of worship. Practice the hymns chosen by the worship committee for use today in the service. The Juniors may be asked to choose a Bible verse for a call to worship, or to learn by heart one chosen by the teacher or the worship committee. Perhaps the chosen memory passage will serve as such a call to worship, or as a response to be given to such a call.

The Worship Service.

QUIET MUSIC.

CALL TO WORSHIP (*read by the worship committee in unison*). (The first and last two verses of Psalm 66 or 67 are excellent for this purpose.)

HYMN. (This may be chosen by the worship committee. The members may need guidance about keeping the thought of Jesus as Leader, and ourselves as followers, in mind as they make their choice, for these two thoughts are the basis of our thought and work together.)

SCRIPTURE READING. (This may be selected from the morning Bible study, or may be a new passage, but the reading may be done by a member of the worship committee.)

MEDITATION: Do you remember how Jesus loved to steal away from the crowds, and even from his friends, to talk to God? Sometimes he spent the whole night on some hilltop, or walking by the sea, talking to his Father in heaven. Always he seemed to come back to his work not only more rested than sleep could have made him but happier and stronger. Many Christians feel that little moments of quiet really help us to know God better. That is because then they can think of God without being interrupted by others' speaking. They can whisper to him how they feel about him, and ask for his help in being good followers of the Lord Jesus. Sometimes they like to listen, to give God a chance to help them to think what he would have them do. Would you like a quiet moment like this, when you can think your own thoughts about God and say to him what you wish? (Thirty seconds is long enough for this sort of experience with children who have never had it before. Stop it immediately by your own prayer if you find that the children are not ready for such an experience yet.)

FOLLOWERS SERVE IN MANY WAYS

PRAYER (*by the leader*). (This should be simple and brief. Make use of happy morning experiences in your thanksgiving.)

HYMN (chosen by the worship committee).

CLOSING PRAYER (*unison*): We thank you, Lord, that you call all who love you your friends. Teach us how to show our love for you. Amen.

QUESTIONS FOR TEACHER AND ASSISTANTS TO THINK ABOUT BEFORE TOMORROW

Are pupil records complete for the school? Are there points that need to be added to individual records because of our work today (see " Keeping Department Records," page 166)?

Were there any problems arising in the work period which call for a discussion period at the very beginning of tomorrow's program?

Are all needed materials available for any new construction plans made by the Juniors today? If not, who will be responsible for getting them here for our work tomorrow?

Are all the committees working smoothly together? Do any of them need time for discussing with the group the necessity for rules about use of play materials, the condition of room or supply cupboards, or ways of improving our worship service?

Are there any other problems?

SESSION 3. FOLLOWERS SERVE IN MANY WAYS

THE TEACHER GETS READY

Read through the suggested procedure which follows. Use it freely in making out your own plan.

If you have never tried getting a group to work out a prayer together, experiment with it as is suggested under " Preparation for Worship."

Note that the worship service suggests a short talk using pictures. Clip from magazines, or borrow from the Primary teacher, three or four pictures of daily workers in both the church and the community. Plan your talk around these; make clear how

God often works for us through people, how he needs our help in making others feel his love and care. Conclude your talk with the thought of Jesus' great concern for people, and how he sent out his followers long ago to help them. You may wish to adapt your worship service by reading from the Bible how he sent out the Twelve to heal and teach and guide others, instead of the Scripture reading now suggested.

Are the questions which concluded the plan for yesterday's program on the previous page the only ones needing your special attention? Do any of the committees, the room committee for instance, require special help? Will you need to provide a planning period before work begins today for the discussion of committee problems? Which committee member or members do you think could best present the problem to the larger group?

A SUGGESTED PROCEDURE

Before school	Memory work
Planning period	Recess
Discussion	Working on records
Bible study	Preparation for worship
Telling or reading a story	Worship service

Before School. Free play under the guidance of the play supervisor. Be sure that the supervisor is familiar with the suggestions under "On the Playground," on page 30. They are there for continued use throughout the school term. It is important that the play period contribute to the Juniors' growth in living together as Christians in the school; this growth will come about as they find better ways of settling differences, insuring good times for all; as they discuss rules and regulations for play; and as they see increasingly the value of fair play and self-control.

Planning Period. This may be a recall of plans and purposes, in connection with any work under way. The Juniors need opportunity to rethink the reasons why they are carrying out their special activities, so that the handwork, or craftwork, will not be something tacked on to the course but will be an integral part of it, a real experience in working as a good follower.

Work Period. Work may be continued on the orange-crate bookcases or supply cupboards if these are being made, on the toy cutouts, dressing dolls, on making a vivarium for some friend who is ill, or on any other construction work planned and begun yesterday. The more the assistant can guide the Juniors in criticizing their own work, the less criticism she will need to give to keep it to a high standard. Guide through thought-provoking questions rather than critical comment. Do not say, " Sandpaper those edges again," but, " How can you tell when the edges are smooth enough for little children to handle? " Do not complain, " Your stitches are much too large and uneven," but ask, " Why is it important to make seams straight? " or: " Does it matter what size we make our stitches? Why? " Make the Juniors exercise their judgment, not merely follow yours.

Discussion. When the Juniors have put away their work materials, call them into an informal discussion group. If the group is not too large the Juniors may gather in a circle about the teacher, or may sit on the floor, or on the grass if there is a suitable shady place for this discussion out of doors. Try to avoid a stiff row-by-row formation for this daily period when the group should draw closer together to share thoughts and experiences.

Perhaps a few minutes will be needed to think again about the questions recorded the first two days: " Have any of them been answered for us through our study and discussion yesterday? [If so, these can be erased, unless groups working on records of discoveries need them.] Are there any new questions for us to think about? [Use your judgment as to whether these can best be handled now in open discussion, or be recorded for future consideration in the light of what you know follows in the course.]

" One important point we discussed yesterday was, ' Who can be a follower of Jesus? ' What did we decide? [It should be clear to every member of the group that anyone who wants to may be Jesus' follower, provided that he really intends to work at it.] We also tried to describe the sort of person we thought would make a good follower or helper. [Be sure that the Juniors are not just responding with what they think you want them to say. Make them give reasons for what they offer; invite others to differ with or expand or qualify the ideas contributed.] Do you think that we must wait until we are ' good enough ' before we can choose to be followers of Jesus? What is the one point about which we must be sure? [That we really want to be his helpers, that we intend to become the kind of helpers that he can use.]

"In our Bible four stories of Jesus have been written down for us by friends of Jesus. Do you suppose that these friends all remembered the very same things about Jesus? Do you suppose that there might have been some things that they all remembered? What sort of things would every follower of Jesus be likely to remember? How do you suppose it happened that some remembered events and sayings that none of the others wrote about?

"Would you like to find some of the special things that these followers of Jesus remembered and wrote about him?"

Bible Study. See that every Junior has a Bible, then assign readings from the following:

Some Stories Found Only in the Gospel of Matthew
Matthew 2:1–12   Matthew 2:13–15, 19–23

"Can you find in these stories what the writer was quoting from his Bible?"

Some Stories Found Only in the Gospel of Luke
Luke 13:10–17   Luke 19:11–28

"What did this writer think Jesus was concerned about?"

Some Stories Found Only in the Gospel of John
John 9:1–12, 34–38   John 13:1–9, 12–17
John 20:30, 31; 21:24, 25

"What sort of friend did this writer think Jesus was? How did he want us to think of Jesus?"

Allow five minutes or more (depending on the reading ability of your group, and their experience in finding Bible references) for quiet study and thought about the questions. Call on each Junior to tell in his own words what he has read, and to give his answer to the question (s) given with his reference. It will be obvious that each reading will make additional contributions to group thinking and help the members to pull their common ideas together into some sort of conclusion.

Ask the Juniors if they would like to look up together one great event that every Gospel writer remembered and thought too im-

FOLLOWERS SERVE IN MANY WAYS

portant to omit from his story. Divide the group in four parts, assigning to each part one of the following references:

Matthew 14:13–21 Mark 6:30–44 Luke 9:10–17
John 6:1–14

Ask some simple fact questions that will help the Juniors to make a common report from the four readings: "How did Jesus and his friends travel together this time? What happened when they reached the other side of the lake? What was their problem as the day grew late? What did Jesus suggest? What did the disciples answer?" When the Juniors have retold their story, ask: "Why do you suppose all the followers remembered this story so well? Why do you think they wanted us to know it?"

Story. "Some Stories Peter Did Not Tell" (see page 119).

Thinking It Through. "Do you suppose John was always as Polycarp knew him? How would you expect being with Jesus to change a young man?

"Think of some people you know who are trying to follow Jesus. What do they do that tells us that they are good followers? In what different ways do they help Jesus? From what we know about Jesus, why can we say that helping others is one way of helping Jesus?"

Material to Memorize. Continue as planned earlier in the week.

Recess (play under the supervision of the assistant in charge).

Working on Records of Discoveries. If there is a lack of variety in the plans which individuals or small groups are making as ways of recording their findings as the course develops, it may be wise to call the group together to discuss the problem. Be sure that they understand that there are many interesting and beautiful ways of keeping such records, and that when they have completed them they will have something worth while to share with one another. If books are being made in one group, other groups should search for other helpful ways of keeping findings. Making posters or planning and making a stained-glass window which will be a record of discoveries about Jesus and what it means to be his follower (see pages 186, 187 for directions) are examples. Grouping picture resources so that they tell a story, or making a special study of one or more of these to see what they tell of followers long ago and now, is still another kind of record. Dramatizing simple incidents in the lives of some of Jesus' followers is still another possibility. Suggestions for dramatization will be found on page 188.

Help the Juniors to feel adventurous about this part of their work; each working group enriches all that the others are doing, and is enriched likewise by the others. If the groups plan new work as a result of this discussion, be sure that they work out the first steps carefully. You will need to be ready to supply information and such material as they cannot secure for themselves. Do these groups realize that any problem which they cannot solve for themselves can be submitted to the larger group for discussion and suggestion?

The worship committee may use part of this period for preparing the worship center, and for preparing those parts of the worship service assigned to them. The committee should begin collecting a variety of worship materials.

Preparation for Worship. Suggest that today the Juniors plan the prayer they will use in the worship service. The following procedure will help such a plan:

" If you were thinking about a prayer to use in our worship service, what do you think ought to go in it? [Write these suggestions on the board as given.] Could we make our prayer better if we rearranged these parts? Which is a good one to go first in our prayer? [Number these as suggested.]

" Do you think we need to reword any of these parts so that they say more clearly exactly what we mean? [The group should work for agreement on final wording.] Do we want to change any of these parts so that they will sound more like a prayer, without changing the meaning? [This may or may not be necessary.] To whom do we make our prayer? How, then, shall we begin our prayer? Shall we read it once more and see if our prayer includes all that we want to say? Does it begin as we want it to? Does it close as we want it to? While you practice the song we shall use today, I will copy our prayer on the board." (This should not be later erased.)

The pianist can take charge of this practice period while the copying is being done.

The Worship Service.
Quiet Music.
Call to Worship. (The worship committee may use the one read yesterday.)
Hymn (chosen by the worship committee).
Scripture Reading. (This may be selected from among the stories told only in Luke's Gospel, as given in the earlier Bible study period, and may be read by a member of the worship committee.)
Talk: Jesus' Many Helpers (with pictures).
Juniors' Prayer (the prayer planned by the Juniors).
Hymn. (Use the new hymn which has been practiced, if it is appropriate at this time, and if it is sufficiently well known.)
Teacher's Prayer: God, our Father, we know you have need of many helpers. We are glad for the many men and women and boys and girls who are following Jesus today; they are your helpers. We too would be your helpers; teach us to serve you well. Bless us now as we go to our homes. May we remember to follow Jesus there as best we can. Bring us together again in the morning, we pray. Amen.

QUESTIONS FOR TEACHER AND ASSISTANTS TO THINK ABOUT BEFORE TOMORROW

Does the possible change in plans for keeping records of discovery call for a beginning planning period tomorrow? Are there other emerging problems or needs which should be talked over by the larger group before beginning work?

Is there a suitable place for the Juniors' unfinished work? Are supplies and working materials where the Juniors themselves can reach them easily?

What additional working materials are needed for work now under way? Are any of these such as could be brought from home by the Juniors themselves?

SESSION 4. GROWING AS FOLLOWERS

THE TEACHER GETS READY

Thus far session plans have been developed in full, with careful suggestions given as to procedure, conducting discussion, helping boys and girls to plan and evaluate their own work, and other details of the Vacation Church School plan. By this time even the new teacher should have experimented with ways of initiating work, guiding discussion, planning for simple worship experiences, utilizing pupil responsibility for the ongoing welfare of the department in all its phases, as has been suggested in previous pages, and in the section "Preparing to Teach This Course" (see page 173).

In the remaining sessions of this unit the teacher will depend more and more on what is happening in her school. Sufficient guidance for session plans is provided here, but the teacher will need to fill in details, and to make needed changes in outline in the light of what is actually taking place in the school. As you read the suggested procedure which follows, try to think of all that has happened thus far in your school and build your own plan accordingly, taking only such help as you may need from the following procedure. Be especially thoughtful as you plan for today's worship service.

A SUGGESTED PROCEDURE

Free play	Recess
Work period	Working on record
Discussion and story	Preparation for worship
Bible study	Worship service

Before School. Free play under guidance of the play supervisor.

Work Period. This may or may not be preceded by a planning period, depending on what happened yesterday (see "Questions for Teacher and Assistants to Think About Before Tomorrow," page 43). The period should be used for work on Junior plans — making cutout toys, dressing dolls, making book covers or posters, making a vivarium, or some other chosen activity. The Juniors should be expected to judge their own work in the light of standards which through guidance they are building for themselves.

Story and Discussion. Again work for informality in the grouping of your Juniors so that they will feel perfectly at home. Try also to see that an increasing number of Juniors take part in the discussion. Avoid all questions that can be answered by " yes " or " no." Encourage real thinking; try not to reveal your own opinions until the Juniors have first had a chance to express theirs. Only the conclusions which Juniors reach themselves will be truly effective in their thinking and acting. Try preceding discussion today with the story. It follows naturally yesterday's discussion. The story is " The Sons of Thunder Learn a New Way " (see page 122).

Some questions which may promote thoughtful discussion follow. Do not try to use them all; do not hesitate to substitute your own questions for any of these proposed:

Yesterday we agreed that being with Jesus might change a young man. Do you remember some points that we made?

Why do you suppose Jesus did not choose older, better men instead of these two hot-headed fishermen? What do you think he found in them that made him want them for friends?

How does one go about trying to live as a follower of Jesus? What does one have to know? to do? If we do not know, how can we find out?

What opportunities are we finding in our school to be good followers? (The play periods give many opportunities for consideration of the rights and wishes of others; the construction work is planned for sharing, or for bringing pleasure or help to others, and so on.)

What did James and John have to learn? How do people grow into better, more dependable helpers?

Looking at Pictures. "Let's look over our pictures and choose four or five that you think will help us to think about what it means to follow Jesus." Appoint four or five Juniors for this, asking them to be ready to give reasons for their choice. While this is being done, have the Bibles distributed, asking those who sit near to take a Bible for the Juniors who are selecting pictures. If there is time left, turn to the unanswered questions on the board to see if any have been answered today.

When the pictures have been brought, let each Junior tell why he has chosen his particular picture. If the pictures are large enough to be seen by the whole group, perhaps they would like to choose one and ask the worship committee to mount it, and use it in the worship center today and tomorrow.

Bible Study. "Suppose we think about the two young men whom Jesus called 'Sons of Thunder.' Would you like to read for yourselves some of the things we heard about them in the story today?"

Assign the following references to small groups. Ask them as they read to decide what the story tells us of these two brothers, and to pick out a verse or two which they think is the very best part of the story. Some Juniors will be asked to read these carefully chosen verses aloud to the group:

Mark 9:38–41	Matthew 26:47–50, 55, 56
Mark 10:35–39, 41–45, 47–50	James 3:13–17
James 1:17, 19, 22	I John 4:19–21
Luke 9:51–56	III John 5, 8, 11

The last three references would best be read by older Juniors; be sure that they understand the few unfamiliar words in these passages. All three passages show how the brothers changed and grew to be worthier followers of the Lord Jesus.

Recess (with play supervisor and game committee in charge).

Working on Records of Discoveries. Continue work as planned yesterday. Help the group to see that what is done by each Junior contributes to the whole group. Take time as needed for discussion of plans and problems.

Preparation for Worship. Discuss with the group ways for making the worship service mean most to the department. Ask those who have gardens at home, or who can gather field flowers, to remember to bring some daily.

Explain to the Juniors that tomorrow the worship committee is to plan the entire worship service and carry it through. What suggestions will they make as to what should go into this service?

Is there something special to think about in that service? What will help to keep this special thought in mind during worship? (Perhaps a picture will be suggested, or a Bible open at the story which speaks of the thing to be kept in mind during worship.) What songs will help the group to think about this idea? Is there some special Bible story among the many heard this week that the Juniors would like to have read again? Will they use the new prayer written yesterday? Will a new call to worship help them to think together as they worship?

This discussion should bring forth enough concrete suggestions to enable the worship committee to prepare and carry through the entire service tomorrow. Meet with the committee as they plan, but be sure they are making their own plan in the light of the group suggestions.

The Worship Service.
QUIET MUSIC.
CALL TO WORSHIP. (Perhaps this ought to be a new one today. If there is time, find one quickly which is linked to the thought suggested by the group for worship tomorrow.)
HYMN (perhaps the new one practiced by the group this week).
STORY (about some missionary or other Christian worker who lives and serves others as a follower of Jesus).
PRAYER (written by the Juniors).
CLOSING HYMN.

SESSION 5. LOOKING BACK AND THINKING AHEAD

THE TEACHER GETS BUSY

Preparation for today's session will depend largely on what happened in school yesterday. Note that today the experiences of the week are pulled together, and all work done is evaluated. The Juniors also should have a large part in planning what is to be done next week. Make yourself familiar with the suggested procedure which follows; even though you do not use this, the elements of the plan can serve as a check list for your own plan.

Note that no new Bible material is suggested. If you plan to re-use the test, be sure that enough copies to go around are ready.

Meet with the worship committee today as they plan their worship service and ways of conducting it. This will be the final contribution of this particular worship committee, as new committees will be chosen today for next week's work.

A SUGGESTED PROCEDURE

Free play
Evaluation of work under way
Work period
Discussion
Repeating the test
Recess
Working on records of discoveries
Election of new committee members
Worship service

Before School. Free play either indoors or out of doors, depending on the weather. The play supervisor will be in charge, assisted by the game committee.

Evaluation of Work Under Way. By this time the orange-crate bookshelves, supply shelves, or cupboards for storing unfinished work should be complete, or nearly so, if these were undertaken. The Juniors who have worked on them should invite the group to inspect them critically. Not only the work, but also how the new storage places are placed for convenience, lighting, and so forth, should be thought about. Any other enterprise under way should be presented to the group for judgment by those who have been working on it. This should include record-making, as well as construction work. The presentation should include not only the work itself, but its purpose, progress, and any problems in connection with completing it about which the workers need the advice and help of the group. Help the Juniors to keep in mind that all activities under way provide them with opportunities to grow as good followers. The way work is planned and carried through, the use to be made of finished projects, reveal whether or not they are growing in their understanding of what a good follower is like.

All thoughtful criticism must be made in the light of definite standards of evaluation. The Juniors may work out some simple standards before work is presented and judged. Following are

LOOKING BACK AND THINKING AHEAD 49

typical questions which promote judgment and good planning, though the Juniors will want to word their own standards. The questions for guiding judgment should be written on the board as the Juniors offer them, in some such fashion as this:

> Is this a good piece of work?
> > Is it neatly done?
> > Is it attractive to look at?
> > Is it useful? In what way?
> Does it meet the purpose for which it was planned?
> > Will it help someone or some group? How?
> > Will it be easy to use as planned?
> > Will its owner be happy to possess and use it?
> How can the work be improved?

If there are problems involved in completing any piece of work, the Juniors should be asked to locate reasons and make suggestions. The following questions will guide constructive thinking:

What remains to be done?
Are Juniors able to handle this?
Are materials lacking?
Where can the workers get these, or what substitutes can be used?
Do problems arise because enough thinking did not precede beginning the work?
If so, what is the best thing to do now?
What about quitting: is it ever justified?

With all incomplete work it is necessary that the workers involved be sure of the next steps. Either the workers should be asked to summarize these or they may ask for advice at this point from the group as a whole. This planning must depend on the work under way and the progress that has been made, but it is an important part of pupil judging.

If any have completed an enterprise today to the satisfaction of the group as a whole, then planning new work is involved. Call on the Juniors to state what the groups should think about as they plan new work. The following points are given as guidance to the teacher as to what is desirable. Bear in mind that the Juniors themselves will think of similar points and express them in their own words. Such Junior proposals, if clear to a whole group and accepted by it, should be recorded on the blackboard for the guidance of groups:

Do we (or someone else) really need or want what we are planning to make?
Is this something worth the time and work involved in the making?
Is this something that we are really interested in making or doing?
Are we able to complete the job if we undertake it? What is involved?
Do we have (or can we get) the necessary materials?
Is there sufficient time left in our school term to complete the work?
Who will be responsible for certain parts of the work? (List these parts and the Juniors responsible.)

Work Period. This should be used in improving the work of groups in the light of the criticisms and suggestions just made.

Informal Discussion and Planning. "One day when Jesus was talking to some of his followers he looked at them and said lovingly, ' Ye are my friends, if . . . ' What do you suppose he included in the words that followed that ' if '? What does it mean to be a real friend?

" Would it be better if it were always easy to be true friends? Explain your answer. Why do you suppose that Jesus still had so many followers in spite of the fact that it is sometimes hard to be a true follower? Does a true follower have to be someone who never makes a mistake? What does a true follower do when he has done wrong? Do you know any ' true followers '? "

Plan with the Juniors ways of discovering more about true followers of Jesus; this was touched upon yesterday. Over the week end the Juniors may interview the pastor, the Sunday School superintendent, or any other church worker, to find out what it means to be a follower of Jesus and who there is in the world and perhaps in the community who is trying to follow Jesus. If you

LOOKING BACK AND THINKING AHEAD

have any books to lend (see book list on page 180), do so and plan to call for reports. Bible references in connection with the Early Church Christians can be used as resource materials also.

Repeating the Test. If the Juniors did not do so well on the test given to them the first day, it would be an interesting experiment to discover whether or not the work of the week has increased their insight as to what it means to be a follower of Jesus. Pass out copies of the very same test again and allow three or four minutes for them to take it. Remember, however, that there are other ways of measuring pupil growth besides their ability to answer these and other questions. Here are some things to watch for if you want to see if your pupils are discovering what it means to live as Christians:

Do they join cheerfully in games not of their own choosing?

Can they accept the criticism of the group and profit by it?

Are they thoughtful in offering criticism and suggestion with a desire to help and not to hurt others?

Do they feel a concern for the welfare and happiness of the group as a whole? Do they try to contribute to this?

Are they increasingly able to take part effectively in committee work or other appointed responsibilities?

Are they growing in the ability to criticize their own work and attitudes?

Is their work often planned for the benefit it brings to others rather than to themselves?

Don't look for a one-hundred-per-cent gain in any of these points, but rejoice if you can see even the slightest improvement or wish to improve in any of these directions. On a Junior level, they all relate closely to what it means to live with our fellow men as Christians.

If the Juniors did well on their tests the first day, write questions 5 and 7 of the test on the board, and ask the Juniors to answer them orally after they have thought about them. Group their statements on the board, and let them criticize these, expanding or changing the wording to improve and complete the thought.

Recess (in charge of the play supervisor assisted by the game committee).

Working on Records of Discoveries. This should be done in the light of criticisms offered earlier by the larger group. The worship committee, which is responsible for the worship service today, may meet during the latter part of this time.

Election of New Committee Members. Following the plan of short-time committees, the Juniors should appoint new members to take the place of those who have been serving this week. Encourage suggestions as to how the new committee members may help more effectively to make the school a satisfactory place in which to live and work. Suggestions, while concrete, should not draw any unpleasant conclusions as to the work of the previous committee members, who were new and inexperienced. Naturally as we grow in experience we learn better ways of working.

The Worship Service (as planned and carried out by the worship committee).

SESSION 6. "YE ARE MY FRIENDS"

THE TEACHER GETS READY

Read through the brief plan before noting at what points you will have to plan in detail. The Bible study period calls for some thinking, so that it will be sufficiently guided. (Note suggestions for this in previous sessions.) The preparation for worship must be planned specifically, while the worship service suggested will need to be changed or replaced in the light of what happens in the preparation period, and in the thinking done by the worship committee. Note that plans for carrying through the service are left to the teacher, in consultation with the new worship committee.

Be sure that the new committees have sufficient help from you to start them to thinking and working independently. This may mean that nothing more is needed than to recall the suggestions worked out by the whole group last week, just previous to the worship service.

If yours is a two-week school, a workers' conference may be needed today to make final plans in the light of the Juniors' decisions as to what is to go into the closing program (for suggestions see page 197). If a three-week or five-week term is planned for, then it is time to work out adaptations of this course (see suggestions on page 14).

A SUGGESTED PROCEDURE

Free play	Bible study
Planning period	Recess
Work period	Work on records of discoveries
Reports and discussion	Preparation for worship
A story to tell or read	Worship service

Before School. Free play.

Planning Period. Thus far the day's work has begun with a work period following outdoor play. Now the pupils know each other well, have had some experience in thinking and planning together, and have adopted certain standards of workmanship. They are now ready to take over an increased amount of responsibility for the work of the school. Thus far the session plan has been made by the teacher and assistants; the Juniors may have real reasons why they would like this changed. They have discovered some new people, some new facts, some new ideas; they will want to do some independent reading about these and perhaps make a study of the picture resources. They may need to be reminded that they are free to come in before school to look at pictures, read books at the table, note on the board their findings or questions they wish to ask in connection with their reading; they may wish that instead of beginning with a planned work period they might have a part of the first morning period for this kind of free activity.

Let the Juniors make any change in order or in the introduction of new program elements *if there are real reasons why the change is desirable*. After discussion they may call on someone to put the new plan on the blackboard.

If the school term is only two weeks in length, use this time to help the Juniors to think about bringing their work to a satisfying conclusion. If they wish an exhibit or a final program for the last day of school, this is the time to begin planning definitely toward that end (see page 197 for suggestions).

Work Period. The Juniors should take advantage of the group suggestions and criticisms made last week.

Reports and Discussion. Call for reports on interviews with grownups over the week end in connection with pupil investigation as to what it means to follow Jesus, and as to living examples of people who are trying to live as Jesus' followers. Missionaries whose work is supported by the local church are sure to be mentioned in this list. Call for reports by those who have been reading to discover more about followers of Jesus.

Recall the last informal discussion in connection with Jesus' words, " Ye are my friends, if . . ." (see page 50). If the group worked out statements of meaning in connection with questions 5 and 7 of the test, these statements should be reviewed and related to week-end investigations and discoveries. Suggestions for stimulating and guiding pupil discussion were given in detail in last week's procedure.

Story. " With One Accord They Continued Steadfast " (see page 125).

Thinking It Through. "If you had been one of that company to whom Jesus said, ' Ye are my friends, if . . .' what would you think this meant for you? " (Perhaps this question should not be answered in words, but the pupils might be given opportunity to think about it before going to the Bible study.)

Bible Study. Stories of Jesus' Steadfast Friends in the Early Church (for study and report and discussion):

> Acts 1:12-14 . Acts 3:1-12, 16
> Acts 2:14, 22-24, 37, 38, 41-46 Acts 4:1-7, 13-22

Explain to the Juniors studying the last reference that the " they " in the story refers to Peter and John, two friends of Jesus, who have just healed a lame man, and are being arrested for daring to follow Jesus openly.

Recess.

Working on Records of Discoveries.

Preparation for Worship. Use this time for the study of a new hymn, or for a planning period in which the worship service of last Friday will be commented upon and plans for this week's worship worked out. Or the Juniors may wish to work out a psalm of praise or a litany to be used in their worship. The procedure is much the same as that suggested on page 42 in connection with the building of a prayer; that is, the Juniors need to be guided to think of actual content, arrangement and wording, and final form of any creative piece of work. The new worship committee may need a few moments of this time in which to set up their new worship center.

The Worship Service.
QUIET MUSIC.
CALL TO WORSHIP:
Leader: Oh, come and let us worship our God!
Junior: Let us bow before him.
SILENT PRAYER.
RESPONSE *(by the Juniors)*:
Hear our prayer, O Lord
And incline our hearts to thee.
HYMN: "Growing Like Jesus," or some other suitable hymn familiar to the group.
PRESENTATION: What It Means to Follow Jesus Today. (Read from the board the statement worked out by the Juniors in connection with answering test questions 5 and 7.)
SCRIPTURE READING: Acts 1:12-24.
POEM: "Following Christ."[1] (Some other selection, as "O Master of the Loving Heart" [see page 62] may be chosen instead.)

>Saviour, in the words I say
>May I follow Thine own way;
>And in all the deeds I do
>Show a spirit fair and true.

>Show me how to play each game
>Fair and square, as in Thy Name;
>Lose the contest if I must,
>But in every act be just.

---

[1] From *Services and Songs for Use in the Junior Department of the Church School,* by Josephine L. Baldwin. Copyright, 1923. Used by permission of Abingdon-Cokesbury Press, publishers.

In my home, at play, at school,
May I keep the Golden Rule;
Bravely face the hardest test,
Love my neighbors, do my best.   Amen.

PRAYER (as previously worked out by the group).
HYMN: "Dare to Be True."
CLOSING PRAYER SENTENCE (*unison*) : O God, our Father, teach us to follow Jesus, our Leader.   Amen.

SESSION 7.   STEADFAST IN DANGER

THE TEACHER GETS READY

Though a suggested procedure follows, it is important that the order of the day suggested by the Juniors yesterday in their planning time be used.

Read carefully the " Note to the Teacher " under " Group Discussion," and plan this period with this particular need of Juniors in mind.   Note suggestions offered and the carefully planned Bible study that follows and enriches this earlier discussion.

Prepare your story carefully, whether it is to be told or read aloud.   It is a dramatic one and should not be spoiled by lack of preparation.

Note that the preparation for worship is left largely to your own planning, though definite suggestions are made for your help.

You will need to arrange early this morning with a small group of Juniors to plan for the presentation of some significant (to them) discoveries gained during their work.   This may be something taken from the records of discovery, or it may be a simple dramatization of some incident (if some group has been working on this), or a short talk or group of talks dealing with " Good Followers " or " What It Means to Be a Follower " or other suitable subject.   (Suggestions for informal dramatization are given on page 188.)

STEADFAST IN DANGER

A SUGGESTED PROCEDURE

Free period	Recess
Work period	Working on records of discoveries
Group discussion	
A story to tell or read	Preparation for worship
Bible study	Worship service

Early Period. Free play, quiet study, picture or music conferences, and so forth as planned by the Juniors yesterday.

Work Period. On any work under way. The Juniors will recall last week's criticisms and suggestions made on unfinished work, and the planning done in connection with new work to be undertaken.

Group Discussion. (Note to the Teacher: The age in which we live is not an easy one in which to grow up. Even young children hear daily over the radio of fear-inspiring events throughout the world. They see war news on the screen and read war stories and other tales of threat and disaster, of man's failure to live at his best and all that this means to his fellows. There is hardly a Junior but has a father or grandfather who fought in the first World War or had to register for the defense of our own country in the later war terror. The only security the child of today knows is the inner security he finds in those who follow the Christ and who therefore cannot be overcome by fear. He needs help in building within himself a like confidence and trust in the Christ we would lead him to follow.)

"Have you ever thought about the things a man must do who wants to be a football star? [The Juniors will be more or less familiar with the rigorous training demanded.] Why wouldn't it be better to save a man's muscles from such hard work? Why not give him all the pies and cakes he wants if he must work so hard on the team? Why cannot so important a man smoke or drink all he wishes? Why send him out to meet a tough opponent in a trial game? Doesn't it seem to be making things unnecessarily hard for him? [Or use the training of a great transport pilot, the grueling hours of practice, the long routine study of instruments, the trial flights alone over mountains and over rough waters.] Does all this not seem to be making things difficult for the people we have to count on? If you were going from

New York to San Francisco, what sort of pilot would you choose to take you there — one who had done all the hard things and met all the tests or one who had been protected from them? Why?

"In choosing helpers for the hardest things, do you think that Jesus needs most those who have had to make hard decisions? Do you think that the way we meet such tests really does something for us? Explain what you mean. Sometimes we come face to face with something that frightens or angers us. The way we meet such tests may be doing something to us."

Story. "Saul Becomes a Follower" (see page 128).

Thinking It Through. "What would you say are the tests of a good follower?" These might be listed on the board, and later added to the record of discoveries. "Do you know another name for 'good follower'?" (Christian, or "like-Christ man.")

Bible Study. How Jesus Trained His Followers:

He asked obedience. Matthew 4:18–22

He taught them. Matthew 5:1–3, 9, 11, 12

He gave them hard work to do. Matthew 10:1–8

He set them an example of courage. Matthew 16:22, 24

He faced danger with them. John 18:1–8, 12

He trusted them. Matthew 28:19, 20a

He promised them help in times of danger. Matthew 28:20b

He warned them against selfishness. Mark 10:43–45

He taught them what love means. John 15:12–17

Ask each Junior to choose one of these passages and to read it carefully to see how Jesus trained his followers and depended on them. The short statement accompanying each passage should be a guide to their reading. In hearing reports call for volunteers and discuss the things Jesus asked of his helpers and what he depended on them for. One of these passages may be chosen by the group for reading in the worship service. They should also choose someone to read it then.

Recess.

Working on Records of Discoveries. There should be some interesting new facts to be recorded as discoveries today. Ask the members of the worship committee to locate a good call to worship and to choose two hymns for the service today, when they withdraw during the latter part of this period with an assistant to prepare the worship center.

Preparation for Worship. See suggestions in connection with yesterday's session and your own plan for utilizing this period. Perhaps part of this period should be used in reviewing the material the Juniors have in their record with a view to planning to make use of it in the final worship program this week, or at the end of short-term schools.

The Worship Service.

QUIET MUSIC.

CALL TO WORSHIP (*led by one or more members of worship committee*).

HYMN (chosen by worship committee).

SCRIPTURE READING (*by Junior*).

SPECIAL FEATURE (prepared by small group using any of the materials or experiences of the unit thus far).

OFFERING, WITH OFFERING PRAYER OR RESPONSE (worked out by the group last week).

HYMN (chosen by worship committee).

CLOSING PRAYER.

SESSION 8. STEADFAST IN DIFFICULTY

THE TEACHER GETS READY

See if you cannot get at least one or two storybooks of Christian heroes. *The Children's Story Caravan* (see bibliography, page 182) would be especially good for use in the study period. Perhaps you would like to choose one of these stories for use in the worship service.

If you have never tried to conduct a memory work period as suggested under "Preparation for Worship," try it today! It can be a very happy and significant experience. Incidentally Juniors will learn more quickly through such a process than they will by a mere repetition of the words.

Your worship committee, and especially those reading the poem, will need your help today in getting ready.

Are there any problems arising out of progressing work (group or committee) that would make a planning period helpful at the very beginning of the session?

A SUGGESTED PROCEDURE

Free period
Work period
Group discussion
A story to tell or read
Bible study
Recess
Working on records of discoveries
Preparation for worship
Worship service

Early Period. To be used in whatever way has been planned by the Juniors, or for individual reading, study, or work, or for group consultation.

Work Period.

Group Discussion. "In our reading two days ago we noticed that over and over the Bible speaks of Jesus' early followers being steadfast. 'Stedfastly in prayer,' 'stedfastly in the apostles' teaching and fellowship,' 'stedfastly with one accord in the temple.' What does 'steadfast' mean? What are some of the times when good followers must be steadfast? Does that apply to long-ago followers only? On what kind of occasion would you expect to find Christians standing steadfast?

"Did anyone ever stand up steadfastly for you when you were needing a friend? Perhaps you can think of a time when someone you knew needed a friend and you either did or did not stand steadfast. [Don't call for incidents; it is enough if Juniors do remember such times.] Our story today is about a friend who was steadfast."

Story. "The Son of Comfort" (see page 131).

Thinking It Through. "Does it ever happen that one who has failed to be steadfast learns how to become so? What's the best thing to do when we feel that we haven't measured up to our standard in steadfastness? Do you remember anything we read in the Bible yesterday that might help a follower at such a time?" (Matthew 28:20b.)

Bible Study. Some People Whose Steadfastness Was Tested:
A man who met the hardest test. Acts 6:8–12; 7:54–59

STEADFAST IN DIFFICULTY

> How steadfast prayer for Peter was answered. Acts 12:1–5, 11–17
>
> Two prisoners hold fast to courage. Acts 16:16–34
>
> Steadfast in danger. Acts 27:1, 2, 14–25
>
> Paul remembers some difficulties he had to meet as a good follower. II Corinthians 11:25–28

If you have books about missionary heroes, or everyday Christian workers, some of the Juniors might go to the reading tables and look these over for incidents about steadfast Christians while the others read their references. Allow plenty of time for finding and reading these longer passages and book references before calling for reports. The group may wish to plan together as to which of these rather significant discoveries concerning the meaning of steadfastness and which examples of steadfast people ought to go in some one or more of the records of discovery that are being made.

Recess.

Working on Records of Discoveries. The Juniors should make use of the supplementary reading done in the Bible study.

Perhaps a part of this time will be needed by committees for caring for their particular responsibilities.

Preparation for Worship. You may begin the study of a special psalm today, one that will fit in well with the unit emphasis. Psalm 121 is a good selection for this study. Talk first to the Juniors about the psalms as hymns of praise and prayer. Jesus and his followers often used such songs and found help in them, though they did not write them. Ask the Juniors to read Psalm 121 (or whatever psalm you have chosen) to see what it is that the author is glad for or is asking of God. Explain any difficult words. Then say: " Many Christians down through the ages, and over all the earth, have loved this song. Can you think why? "

Tell the Juniors that you could think of no more beautiful gift to give them than to give them this psalm for their very own, and that, although you cannot do this, you can and will be glad to give them two quiet minutes today and each remaining day of the week in which they can learn as much of this lovely old song as they can master. It has been found that this method of privilege is far more effective than setting down a certain number of verses to memorize in drill periods of three times the length allowed here. Close the learning period by inviting the group to repeat softly together as much as they have learned; allow them to look at their open Bibles today if they need to. Try to emphasize the beauty of the psalm and the fact that we may have it for our own; do not drill for exact wording today. That will come through use later.

The Worship Service.

QUIET MUSIC.

CALL TO WORSHIP (as planned by worship committee).

HYMN (selected by worship committee).

SCRIPTURE READING (*repeated together slowly and thoughtfully*): Psalm 23.

POEM: "O Master of the Loving Heart"[1] (*read by four Juniors*). (This may, but need not, be by members of worship committee.)

> O Master of the loving heart,
>   The Friend of all in need,
> We pray that we may be like Thee
>   In thought and word and deed.
>
> Thy days were full of kindly acts,
>   Thy speech was true and plain;
> And no one ever sought Thee, Lord,
>   Who came to Thee in vain.
>
> Thy face was warm with sympathy,
>   Thy hand God's strength revealed;
> Who saw Thy face, or felt Thy touch,
>   Were comforted and healed.
>
> O grant us hearts like Thine, dear Lord,
>   So joyous, true, and free,
> That all Thy children everywhere
>   Be drawn by us to Thee. Amen.

HYMN (chosen by worship committee).

PRAYER OR RESPONSE (as worked out by the group last week).

MIZPAH BENEDICTION. (This can be written on the board if it is not familiar to the Juniors.)

---

[1] By Calvin W. Laufer. Copyright, 1927.

SESSION 9. WHEN IT IS HARD TO CHOOSE
THE TEACHER GETS READY

Don't forget to keep the Juniors' own plans foremost.

The discussion will be stimulating if the leader does not use it as a chance to "preach at" the children Be content to use some of the questions proposed for the purpose of stimulating Junior thinking, and not as a chance to "get back the right answers." This is particularly true when it comes to trying to work out a simple test to be used in evaluating the choices people make.

Work hard on the story; it is worth the effort.

Note that in the "Preparation for Worship" you have an opportunity to make up your own original story out of the material provided there.

The worship service today is to be planned by the worship committee and you, conferring together. By this time a wealth of new materials and ideas has been gathered, and the planning for the service ought to be a rich experience. It can be done during the work period following immediately after recess. Work with any other committees that may be assisting in the group; be ready at all times, not to solve their problems for them, but to help them to face these and work out their own solutions. Suggestions for doing this have been provided earlier.

If tomorrow is the final day for your school of two weeks, you will need most of the session today to prepare for tomorrow. Read again the suggestions on page 197.

A SUGGESTED PROCEDURE

Free period	Recess
Work period	Work period
Group discussion	Preparation for worship
Bible study	Worship
A story to read or tell	

Early Period. As planned by the Juniors. Doubtless some of this time will be needed for critical evaluation of work and planning tomorrow's program if your school closes then. Time for problem discussion and large or small group consultation should always be possible whenever needed before going on to a new day's work.

Work Period.

Group Discussion. If the Juniors used the early period for consultation this morning, recall what happened. Why was discussion necessary? What choices had to be made? What helped the group or the individual workers to make good choices of materials or procedures for carrying on their work? (If there was no such beginning period, recall some recent one.)

" Let's think about other times when men and women and boys and girls have to make choices. What is going on in the world today that tells us that some people are making choices? Think of some of the helpful things that are being done in our town; who chose to have these things done? Why? Do you know anyone in — [home town] whom you would call a wise chooser? Why? What makes his choosing good?

"Are there times in school when you have to make hard choices? Would you like me to list on the board examples of times when we have to make choices? [Let the Juniors suggest these.]

" Why do you suppose God has made it necessary for us to make choices every day? Why did he not decide everything for us? Would that make it easier for us and for him? [Face the fact that it undoubtedly would, then help the Juniors to try to think why God wants us to do our own choosing.] God did make some things that can never choose for themselves. The sun never chooses to give its light each day. The mountains never choose where they will stand. The sea never chooses its tides. Can the mountains love God? How does love prove itself? Do you remember a test Jesus suggested to his followers by which they could test their love for him as their Leader? " (If the Juniors do not recall it, ask them to read together John 14:15.)

Bible Study. Assign or call for volunteers on the following passages to be read and reported:

>Jesus tells three stories of choices. Matthew 13:44; Matthew 13:45, 46; Matthew 13:47, 48
>
>A young man chooses badly. Matthew 19:16–22

WHEN IT IS HARD TO CHOOSE

A sinner chooses wisely. Luke 19:1–8

Jesus' followers make their choice. Mark 10:28–30

Thinking It Through. "What makes a choice good or bad? What help do we have in making wise choices? Would you like to list on the board some ways by which we can test a choice?" (These may be in the form of questions; for example: Does this choice make it easier for others to choose wisely? Does it help my group to carry out its purpose? and so forth.)

Story. "Barnabas Stands By" (see page 134).

Recess.

Work Period. On records of discoveries, or on other Junior plans which need extra time.

Preparation for Worship. If there is, among the pictures that you have bought or clipped or borrowed, a picture showing the Boy Jesus on the way to Jerusalem or a picture of the pilgrims at the Jerusalem gate, it may be put on display. Such pictures can often be borrowed from the public library. Tell in your own words the story of the pilgrims who once a year gather at dawn in the northernmost parts of the land to start their long journey to the great feast at Jerusalem. Here stands their glorious Temple, where once a year the people love to gather together to worship God as a nation. Families meet their friends and relatives as they journey, and every crossroads finds new pilgrims waiting eagerly to join the band. Tell of the night camps, of the stories the old men tell and the boys listen to with breathless attention. Picture the great company, growing greater every hour, as the pilgrims march singing across the plains and around the lake and over the hills. Tell how eagerly they watch for the first gleam of the Temple's shining dome and how joyfully they point it out to the littlest ones. Then describe the mighty song that rings out across the hills round about Jerusalem as everyone joins in:

> "I will lift up mine eyes unto the hills
> From whence cometh my help."
> (Psalm 121, King James Version.)

Try to help the Juniors to see what this song meant to the Temple pilgrims, and still means to all who love God and seek to worship him. Let them read the whole song aloud from their Bibles (Psalm 121) and recall how much they learned of it yesterday. Offer them a new quiet two minutes to learn what more of it they can. Let the psalm be repeated softly together, and suggest that if they wish, they may use the psalm at their final weekly service tomorrow.

Plan in general for the worship tomorrow in the whole group now, as was done last week (see suggestions for tomorrow's service given on page 69). The worship committee, with a minimum of guidance, can be trusted to take over group suggestions as the members assume responsibility for tomorrow's service.

The Worship Service. Plan this yourself, in conference with the worship committee, using some of the new materials and ideas gained thus far during the school term.

SESSION 10. GROWING DEPENDABLE [1]

THE TEACHER GETS READY

(Review the period for evaluation of work and the planning of new work as suggested on pages 48–50.) Use this as guidance material in planning the first part of the session today.

Note that no new Bible or story material is offered for today. The Juniors need time to relive some of their past experiences and to evaluate their work and their school. They need time to think ahead and to plan for the new unit, and to elect new committees.

Preparation for worship calls for some careful work on your part. Keep the period very informal; do not allow a solemn tone to spoil this friendly, intimate period.

Think ahead as to the possibilities that the members of the worship committee can seize upon in their planning today. Leave just as much of the responsibility to them as they can carry effectively, but do not allow them to feel overwhelmed or at a loss as to what they have to do.

[1] The following plan is prepared for ongoing schools. For schools of two weeks, a special program planned by the Juniors will be given today. Suggestions for this were given on page 197.

In the planning period before election of new committees it may be wise to ask the group to think about the work done by the committees during the week. Do not encourage personal or unfriendly criticism of individual committee members, but aim to lead the Juniors in thinking about what was done and how it helped them in their work. Out of the positive criticisms helpful suggestions for still further improvement of work, so that it will make group activity easier and happier, will be received with appreciation. Then elect the new committees who the members of the group think can thus add to their convenience in the use and care of room and supplies, or in making a better use of the playground or of the worship period.

A SUGGESTED PROCEDURE

Planning period
Work period
Discussion
Recess
Working on records of discoveries
Preparation for worship
Worship service

Planning Period. Suggestions for the evaluation and criticism of work were given in Session 5. Use these today for all work under way, or for the planning of new work.

Work Period. The Juniors will keep in mind suggestions made by the whole group at the earlier period.

Discussion. " What are some of the things that we have been thinking about during our school? [The session titles offer one way of recalling some of these.] Shall we take time to look through our records of discoveries to see what we have added? Suppose we list on the board some ideas that we think worth keeping in mind after our school is over. John, will you write on the board something that you think is important enough for us to hold fast? [Let three or four others do this if they volunteer; do not try to determine what things shall be chosen.]

" What stories did you like best? What Bible readings have you thought of most often? Is there some part of our worship that you especially liked or wished that we might improve? How can we do this? Are there some special things that you think we should keep in mind as we look ahead to next week's work?

" Next week we shall begin a brand-new unit. So far we have

thought chiefly of the followers of Jesus about whom we read in our Bibles. Are all Jesus' followers to be found in Bible stories? Where else would you look for them? How can we get information about Jesus' followers today? Suppose that over the week end we see what we can find out about what it means to be Jesus' follower now. Perhaps we shall discover someone right in our own community who we think is trying to follow Jesus right now. Shall we see if we know someone like that?"

If you have some of the books in the list on page 182, which tell of modern Christian leaders, you might offer to lend one or more of these books to volunteers who can be trusted to do some reading and report, and who will take care of the book so that the whole group will not lose the use of it. It may be wise to indicate several possible choices for such reading.

Recess.

Working on Records of Discoveries. While the larger group is at work on the records, the worship committee can retire with you or an assistant and plan for the worship service. Suggestions for this were offered yesterday during "Preparation for Worship." Do not use the program of worship which follows if the members of the group are ready to work out their own without its help. If you feel that they do need aid in getting started, use only such parts of it as may be needed to stimulate ideas for their own planning. If anyone brought flowers or a special picture, be sure that these are used in the planning. If the members of the worship committee wish to call in other Juniors to take part in the service rather than doing all the leading themselves, encourage them to do so.

Preparation for Worship. By this time the Juniors have been worshiping together long enough to begin to think of some of the real values to be got out of true worship. These will not be expressed as you would express them (unless you have let the Juniors fall into the lazy way of giving back to you what they think you want them to say or do) but they ought to be thoughtful suggestions, having value for the group. Perhaps you might start such a discussion by asking: "Why do you think the pilgrims looked forward each year to meeting together in the beautiful Temple in Jerusalem? Was it just because they liked to meet their friends again? What else happened in Jerusalem at this happy meeting time? Why do you suppose they *liked* to worship in the great Temple? [The Juniors may know of the great beauty of the Temple itself, and of the choirs and priestly bands of musicians who added something to the service, or it can be pictured for them. You can also lead them to see that there was something about coming together and thanking God for his love and goodness, offering him gifts, and speaking to him in their hearts, that made them feel sure that they had a mighty Friend to whom they could speak at any time. Even Juniors can understand how true worship means a time of companionship with God, either with others or alone; they can appreciate in some degree the genuine happiness and security that God's people feel when they know that he is their Friend and that they can approach him with confidence in his love for them.

" [Ask them to see if the pilgrim song (Psalm 121) which they have been learning tells us anything of what worship meant to the pilgrims, and what God meant to them as they worshiped him.] What does this song tell us about God? What does it tell us about the way the pilgrims felt about him? Is this song still one that people who worship God can sing? Would you like another two or three quiet minutes in which to learn the rest of it? "

The Worship Service.

QUIET MUSIC (planned with the pianist by the committee).

CALL TO WORSHIP (selected by committee and read by one of its members).

HYMN (selected by committee).

A SONG OF PRAISE (*in unison, from memory if possible*): Psalm 121.

REPORT: Following Jesus by Being Friendly (a Junior report summarizing ways in which Jesus' followers can show friendliness to others).

REPORT: Following Jesus by Being Steadfast (a Junior report summarizing times when followers need to stand firm as good followers).

REPORT: Following Jesus by the Choices We Make (a Junior report summarizing ways in which we can judge our choices).

PRAYER (*by a Junior, or by some assistant whom the committee has called upon*): Father, we would be dependable helpers. May we remember that, as we live with others in home and school and neighborhood, we have opportunities to be friendly and helpful. Grant that we may not forget that in the choices we make each day we can honor you. Make us always steadfast and true, helpers you can really depend upon. We ask it in our Leader's name. Amen.

CLOSING HYMN (chosen by the committee).

Unit II. Each in His Own Way

SESSION 1. WHAT CAN A GOOD FOLLOWER DO?

THE TEACHER GETS READY

Plan I. For Ongoing Schools.

1. This is the beginning of a new unit. Though independent of Unit I, "'Ye Are My Friends,'" it follows naturally after it. Note the suggestions for free examination and discussion of new materials under the leadership of assistants which is planned for the beginning of the session. If you use assistants, put one in charge of each of the tables and see that each has access to the procedure which concerns her under "A Suggested Procedure." You will pull the experiences together in the discussion that follows the game.

2. A game is needed after the work at the tables, and it should be planned by the play supervisor if you have one.

3. Speak in advance to one of your assistants so that she will be ready to take notes as the Juniors discuss ways of being a good follower. If the discussion must be held indoors, these points can be listed immediately on the board as the Juniors suggest them. Otherwise, they may be noted down on paper and transferred later.

4. If possible, get a print of Rodin's *Cathedral*. It can be obtained in size 5 x 7 inches for 25 cents (glossy prints, 50 cents) and postage at the Rodin Museum, Twenty-second Street and Parkway, Philadelphia, Pennsylvania. While it is not absolutely necessary in view of the full explanation given, the Juniors will be interested in seeing it.

5. The important thing today is that the members of the group shall begin consciously to think about the fact that there is no one way or "best way" of being a good follower of Jesus. They should begin to appreciate that anyone who wishes to may be a

good follower, " each in his own way." The Juniors will think of many ways by which people have served Jesus, have shared the story of his love and life with others all through the years, but the emphasis in this unit is not on what has been done (except by way of illustration and appreciation) but on the fact that we all can do something as his dependable followers if we will.

6. By this time the group will have had some experience with committees and perhaps as members of committees. Don't forget that the new committees will still need some help and encouragement from you at first and that today is their first day in office.

7. In planning their new work after recess encourage the Juniors to examine carefully supplies on hand as they make up their list of needed materials and before they ask individual Juniors to bring additional materials or you to purchase them. The activities selected should be quite different from those worked on during the first unit.

8. If you plan a missionary emphasis for Sessions 6 and 8, write *immediately* to your missions headquarters for story material.

Plan II. For Schools Just Beginning.

1. Read carefully the sections " Planning for Your Own Vacation School," page 13, and " General Plans for Conducting the Department," page 165. If you are planning to work with Junior committees, page 171 will be of special interest.

2. Read the plan for Session 1, Unit I, beginning on page 18, for suggestions about enrolling the pupils the first morning, and for preliminary activities.

3. Browse through the questions following the end of the first few session plans in Unit I; they deal with the kind of questions you must face with your assistants in the ongoing work of the school.

4. If you are using assistant teachers, be sure the assistant in charge of playground has access to the suggestions found in Session 2, Unit I, page 30.

5. Read through the session plan suggested for today. Be sure that you know exactly what you are working toward as you plan for this first day. You will want to read points 2, 4, and 8 under Plan I, as they concern you also.

6. Assistants should have access to the plan for table displays,

WHAT CAN A GOOD FOLLOWER DO?

questions to be listed on blackboard or at tables, and suggestions for guiding the discussion. If there are not enough assistants for you to set up four tables as suggested in the procedure, one or two tables can be used and a combination made of the displays and the discussion questions, selecting those items and questions which are most helpful in the light of available resources and the experience of your Juniors.

A SUGGESTED PROCEDURE

As the Juniors arrive, invite them to examine the books, pictures, or objects attractively displayed on tables. There should be an assistant in charge of each table.

For the Bible and Hymnal Table. Have several Bibles, perhaps one of them Moffatt's Translation, open at The Psalms. Have several church hymnals also on display, open at the very oldest hymns, such as any of the following. (Two Juniors may share a hymnbook if necessary.)

"O Gladsome Light, O Grace" — Greek, third century or earlier.

"O Splendor of God's Glory Bright" — Ambrose of Milan, fourth century.

"Christian, Dost Thou See Them" — Andrew of Crete, eighth century.

"All Glory, Laud, and Honor" — Theodulph of Orleans, ninth century.

"Jerusalem the Golden" — Bernard of Cluny, twelfth century.

Put on the board the following questions to guide the Juniors as they read these ancient hymns of praise:

Who or what is spoken of in this ancient hymn?
What is the hymn trying to tell us about this?
Find one phrase that you like and understand. What does it mean?
Why do you think the author used elsewhere such odd phrases?
If he were writing today instead of centuries ago, how might he reword some of the phrases?
Find another hymn that you like on the same theme as this one.

In guiding conversation at the table, keep the following facts in mind: Language has changed much in the centuries since these hymns and psalms were written. They are all hymns of praise of God, Christ, or heaven, save Andrew of Crete's hymn, which is a warning to resist temptation. What is true of the ancient hymns is likewise true of the meaning and purpose of the psalms, which are all prayers to and praise of God. It will be necessary to help the Juniors to locate familiar ideas, and to guide their thinking as they try to express these same ideas in their own everyday language, or as they search for another praise hymn. Try to help the Juniors to find real beauty and love for Christ in these quaint old songs which are so different from our modern hymns. Suggest that perhaps in ages to come children will find difficult and different the very hymns we love today, even though they may still be happy in their service to the same Lord Jesus.

For the Book Table. If possible, have on display any of the following books:

The Secret, by Harold Burdekin.
The Story of Our Bible, by Harold Hunting.
Far Round the World, by Grace W. McGavran.
The Friendly Missionary, by Nina L. Millen.

If you have none of these, try to display any books, magazines, or illustrated papers which contain stories of Christian service in this or other lands; books of retold Bible stories; books containing pictures, poems, or prayers about our beautiful world, or that relate the world to God, its Creator.

Write on the board the following questions to guide Junior thinking as these books are examined:

Why do you think the author wrote this book (or story or poem)? Why is this a good purpose?

Could you say this book might be the author's way of serving God? How?

If you were a follower of Jesus and able to write a good book, name several kinds of books you might write. How would such books help others?

Be sure the reading materials you select are simple enough for Juniors to understand, so that they can discuss the author's pur-

WHAT CAN A GOOD FOLLOWER DO?

pose. Help them to look for special things in the book besides the author's purpose — an attractive picture to share, a good quotation to read, a brand-new idea beautifully expressed, a new fact worth remembering.

For the Picture Table. On the picture table, have as many of the pictures listed on page 183 as you can manage. It is most desirable that there be at least two or three of the early primitives, such as Cimabue, Giotto, Taddeo Gaddi. Try to get at least one picture by Fra Angelico, of whom we shall be hearing later in the course. If you cannot get a good display of these prints, clip the best pictures of Jesus you can find from old Sunday School materials. If possible, try to have pictures which have been painted by artists from various countries. *Each with His Own Brush,* by Daniel J. Fleming, would be a rich addition to your picture resources for this unit, or either of the inexpensive little volumes, *The Life of Jesus,* selected and arranged by Myrtle K. Wilde (see page 183). If you must depend on your own clipped or borrowed pictures, mount these attractively. If your church has a stereopticon machine or slide projector, plan to show some carefully chosen pictures on the life of Christ as painted by various artists (see pages 184, 185 for sources for this).

The assistant in charge of the picture table should help the children to watch for artists' names and dates in looking at pictures. The dates will explain much about the pictures. For example, artists in Giotto's day did not know about foreshortening and perspective. They tried to show distant figures by making them smaller. They did not know about body bones and structure and so drew hands and necks and feet much as children draw them. They did not know how to make shadows well. But all their pictures of Jesus contain great and beautiful ideas and Juniors can be guided to see and appreciate these. In the days when the ancients painted, men and women could not read unless they were very, very rich, for there were no schools for poor people; books had to be painted or written by hand, for there were no printing presses. These pictures of Jesus were the only way people had of following the story of Jesus' life and works, for even when their leaders read from the Bibles, they read in Latin, a language the people could not understand. Help the Juniors to see how many lands through their many artists have enriched our thinking about Jesus, and have shown us what Jesus has meant to them and their people.

If you have any of these early pictures, write the following questions on the board as a guide to thinking and discussion; if you are depending on more recent pictures, use only the last three questions:

Are all these pictures equally beautiful? Why or why not?

Can you think why the earliest of these painters might not have been able to make pictures so lovely as could the later painters?

Do you think the early painters should not have tried to paint Jesus until they could do it perfectly?

If they had not, what would the people of their day have lost?

Find a picture of Jesus or his followers that you particularly like.

What is the artist trying to tell us? Why do you like this picture?

What do you think would be a good title for this picture?

The Objects Table. Plan this carefully; every object should suggest service for Christ by those who would be his real followers. Perhaps there is a beautifully embroidered bookmark in the pulpit Bible that you can borrow or a lovely vase usually found filled with flowers for the worship service in your church. These have been made or given by someone who knew the importance of the Bible to us, and the beauty of worship. An offering envelope or a collection plate, a Bible translated into some other language than our own, a set of workman's tools, a framed picture of a child helping — any of these and other objects you will think of all suggest the value of service done honestly and in the spirit of Jesus. The following questions written on the board will guide pupil thinking and discussion:

What do these objects suggest to you about ways of being good followers?

Why has someone made or given these beautiful things used in our worship?

Find some special object that suggests a kind of service you especially like.

WHAT CAN A GOOD FOLLOWER DO?

What sort of work must be done by these tools if they are really used to honor the workman's Leader?

Name at least three other objects that might be put here to remind us of good ways of serving Jesus. Be ready to tell why you thought of them.

This examination period should proceed in an unhurried manner. The Juniors should understand that while working in various groups, they are all gathering information and ideas about the various ways of serving him which the followers of Jesus have found.

A Game. When the groups have completed their examination suggest that they play a brief game in or out of doors. They may then come together, preferably out of doors in some shady place, for a discussion of the question, What does a good follower do?

Discussion. Ask someone to recall the question that we are to think about today (see the session title). If this is not the first day of school, the Juniors will have a good deal of background about followers of Jesus and ways of showing love for him. If this is the first day of a new term, take a few moments in which to help the Juniors to recall something about Jesus and his followers of long ago. Remind them that Jesus invited anyone who wished to to become his follower and helper. Let the Juniors think of people in their community who they feel are trying to follow Jesus today. Juniors in ongoing schools may be ready to report on week-end interviews and investigations. Suggest that the Juniors list ways of helping Jesus. They will be sure to mention being missionaries, being ministers, or some other phase of familiar Christian service supported by the church.

" Once a great artist wanted to remind people that Jesus said, ' Where two or three are gathered together in my name, there am I.' He did it by carving something out of stone which he called ' *Cathedral.*' What do you suppose he carved? [The Juniors will doubtless suggest a church building of some kind unless they know Rodin's *Cathedral*, which is merely a picture of two hands joined in prayer. Explain that it is only those who look closely who can really understand the artist's message, because the artist carved, not the hands of one person clasped in prayer, but two right hands joined in prayer.] What does that say to you? [If you do not have the picture of Rodin's *Cathedral,* let the Juniors join their right hands together as though they were clasped in prayer. Help the Juniors to catch the idea that two friendly hands joined together in worship, work, or kindness, and the promise of Jesus' presence can make any place where even two Christians meet a real church. Call on someone to read Matthew 4:20]. Do you think that artist might have found a way to serve men with such a message in stone? Explain your answer."

Ask someone who worked with the objects at the table to bring something from that table that suggests a way someone found or can find to follow Jesus. Let him explain. Call on the Juniors from the book table, the picture table, the hymnal table, to tell what they found out about different ways of being good followers. Call on any who are ready to enrich the growing list of ways of serving Jesus which we have discovered. If, in ongoing schools, some Juniors took books home to read of Christians who have shown what it means to be a good follower, let them report on their reading. Invite an assistant to make a record of ways in which the Juniors feel we may follow Jesus and to copy them on the board later for a permanent record.

"We have talked about people who showed love for Jesus by writing hymns of praise about him. Long before Jesus came men wrote psalms of praise to God to show their love for him. We found that artists have painted their best pictures of Jesus to remind us of all that he did for us. We looked at some books that said to us: 'Jesus is important, the greatest of all leaders. He can be trusted if we decide to follow him, and these are some ways we may serve him.' The authors of such books have found a way of serving Jesus themselves. Can you think how? Do you think we have named all the ways there are of serving Jesus?"

Reading from the Bible. Call on someone to pass Bibles around, and ask the Juniors to find and read, first silently and then together, Matthew 25:34–40. "Many of us cannot write books or paint pictures or be missionaries in far places. Do you think Jesus is trying to say something to those of us who cannot do something great for him? What?" (The least of us has something to share with others, if no more than an act of friendliness.)

Story. "Our story today is about a prisoner. Would you

think that there was anything a prisoner could do to be one of Jesus' helpers?" Tell the story, "A Prisoner Finds a Way to Help," on page 136.

Thinking It Through. "What is it that makes a good follower of Jesus? Can people who have great wealth and great skill and great brains follow him? What can they do? Can people who have little money and no great talent follow him? How? Our new unit is called 'Each in His Own Way.' What do you think that means?"

Recess. Suggestions for making use of play experiences in developing Christian ways of living in the school will be found on page 30 in Unit I.

Planning Our New Work. Call attention again to the title of our unit. Let the Juniors suggest the sort of things we shall be thinking about in our school during the next two weeks. Suggest that some of us will be most interested in discovering what others have done as good followers of the Lord Jesus. Some of us will be interested in making use of what some good followers have done for us, through learning to appreciate and interpret their pictures, songs, and poems, which make Jesus real to us. Some of us may wish to plan some very definite ways of being good followers by helping others. Discuss possibilities with the Juniors (many suggestions for all sorts of activities are offered on page 193). They may divide into groups according to their interests for planning their new work under the leadership of assistants. Perhaps the groups will get little farther today than planning, but that planning should include such items as an exact statement of the work to be done, listing materials needed and how to secure these, and division of work. This planning period should also include the making of a report tomorrow morning to the group as a whole.

If yours is a new school, the last part of the period before the preparation for worship should be used for the election of committees (see page 171 for suggestions) and for the instruction of the committees by the group as to what we shall be looking for in the way of service from them. The group should also discuss ways and means of co-operation with their committees, accepting the fact that the committees cannot bear sole responsibility for the welfare of the school but will need the help of all.

Preparation for Worship. Discuss ways by which men worshiped God and still worship him. Worship through song, prayer, reflection on God's love and care of us, appreciation of and right use of his good gifts to us, joyous service with him and for him are outstanding means of worship which the Juniors will suggest under your thoughtful guidance.

Speak briefly of the parts of our worship service and their purpose in helping us to worship — the quiet music which prepares us to think together of God and to get ready to worship him, and so on through the various parts of the service.

The Worship Service. The worship for this unit will be built around the thought of serving Jesus as his followers or helpers. Each plan should, of course, be adapted freely in the light of all that happens during each session, for true worship is and must be an outgrowth of experience rather than a matter of a nicely arranged program put down on paper. These programs are offered for whatever suggestion they may give to the teacher and the Junior worship committee, which is responsible for planning worship; the suggestions will fail in their purpose if they are adopted "as is" without thought about what is happening from session to session. The worship committee should take an increasingly significant part in planning and carrying out the worship.

QUIET MUSIC.

CALL TO WORSHIP: Any familiar Bible verse or hymn stanza about worship, praise, or thanksgiving to God. (Schools completing the first unit may wish to use the psalm learned last week as a unison reading from memory.)

PRAYER: We are young, our Father, but it is very wonderful to us that you planned a world in which boys and girls can truly help you as followers of the Lord Jesus. We ask that you will show us ways of working with you, ways in which we can help you to carry out your good plans for our world. We ask this in our Leader's name. Amen.

HYMN: " Growing like Jesus " (Hymn 82 in *Hymns for Junior Worship,* or a hymn of similar emphasis from whatever hymnal you are using).

STORY: " Christians Are Different."

A short time ago a traveler wrote of an interesting experience that had happened to her:

She was traveling in Palestine and was being driven by an Arab chauffeur. On the road there was a man — a Jew — who was having serious car trouble.

The Arab stopped and tried to help with the car, but did not have the parts needed to repair it. So the Jew was invited to get into the Arab's car and ride to a garage for help.

After the man had been left at the garage and the party was on its way again, the traveler expressed surprise at the Arab's kind treatment of the Jew. "I did not know that Arabs were so friendly to Jews," the traveler said.

The Arab answered, "Oh, but I am a Christian."

HYMN or POEM (about service or working with God).

CLOSING PRAYER.

SESSION 2. GOOD FOLLOWERS HAVE GIVEN US OUR BIBLE

THE TEACHER GETS READY

The various tables used yesterday should be used again today, and during the rest of the week. Junior groups should rotate from table to table, selecting a new one each morning for examination and study. Note particularly the plan to enrich displays by inviting the Juniors to contribute to them. Encourage the Juniors to bring in Bibles or hymnals in other languages for use on the Bible or hymnbook table. Take some responsibility yourself for further enrichments of the displays.

Be careful today to find out what the Juniors know of the ways through which our Bible has come to us; it is a good plan to draw information from the Juniors rather than to tell them everything.

Note the plan for reporting and studying group plans as a whole before the work period gets under way. Such planning periods are a significant part of your session program where you are providing genuine opportunity for Christian living in your school. Pages 31 and 33 of Unit I offer detailed suggestions for reporting on and discussing group work plans.

You may need to secure special working materials to meet special plans of the group; there should be those materials which the Juniors themselves cannot furnish.

Will the new worship committee need help in planning a worship center? (If you are just beginning a new school, read over plans for this in Sessions 1 and 2 of Unit I.)

If your school is in a community where the Juniors are not likely to have Bibles at home, investigate the possibility of providing each Junior with a copy of one of the Gospels or the book of The Psalms. These cost as little as two cents each. Write to the American Bible Society, Bible House, Park Avenue and Fifty-seventh Street, New York City.

A SUGGESTED PROCEDURE

Examining Table Displays. Let the Juniors again examine the various table displays, as was suggested yesterday. Groups should work at other tables than the ones visited yesterday. Some new questions may be added to those already listed; these should grow out of yesterday's discussion in the larger group.

Discussion. Begin with an invitation to the Juniors to report any new and interesting findings made at the tables, or to ask any questions about these. Objects may be brought from any of the tables for examination. Discussion should always be related to facts these various objects suggest of ways men have found to follow Jesus through service to him and to their fellow men. The worship service of yesterday should provide clues for enriching this discussion.

Invite the Juniors to bring various contributions from home for use on any of the tables. These should be regarded as "loan exhibits," and plans for their care, use, and safe return should be worked out by the group as a whole.

Introduction to the Story. Hold your own Bible, or call attention to the one at the worship center. "Long ago our Bible was not written in our own language. It was written in strange tongues that only the learned could read. People could not understand the words of Jesus, nor the story of his love and help, because they did not understand the words the priests read. They had to depend on pictures their artists made in paint or in stone.

GOOD FOLLOWERS HAVE GIVEN US OUR BIBLE

These were all they had to tell them what they wanted to know about Jesus.

"Then came a good and learned Englishman named John Wycliffe who knew and loved the Bible very dearly. It grieved him that his countrymen could not know what it had to tell them of God's love and of Jesus who came to show that love. He decided to do a very wonderful thing. [If any Junior knows of John Wycliffe's work of translation, let him tell it to the group. If none know, tell briefly of John Wycliffe's painstaking care in translating the Bible into English, and of his writing it out word by word with his own hand, for printing presses had not yet been invented in the fourteenth century.]

"John Wycliffe helped to give the Bible to us, but he was not the first who helped. Do you know who else helped?" (If the Juniors have little background, help them to see how the disciples of Jesus kept the story alive, telling it over and over so that men would not forget it; how men wrote it down in Greek and other languages and cared for the writings, reading them in their homes, and at their worship services. Tell how men protected the Bible for us with their lives, often dying rather than surrendering the Bible to the men who wanted to destroy it. Explain how Gutenberg and his printing press made it possible for Bibles to be made more cheaply than the handwritten Bibles, because it took the copyists so long to write them out word by word. Ask the Juniors to be thinking of other ways by which the followers of Jesus have helped to give our Bible to the world; this will be discussed further during preparation for worship this morning.)

Story. "A Costly Gift Is Our Bible," see page 139.

Finding Special Stories and Poems in Our Bibles. Pass out Bibles to the Juniors and invite them to suggest Bible stories, psalms, or verses that they especially like. Help them to locate some of these and to read them. Try to call on the Juniors who read with some ease to do the reading aloud, while the others follow the story in their Bibles. Perhaps the Juniors will want to take a few moments in which to read again and to memorize the passage read yesterday (Matthew 25:34-40).

Thinking It Through. "If someone asked you how Jesus' followers who gave us our Bibles have helped to make this a better world, what would you say?" (List these answers.)

Recess.

Reporting on Work Plans. Before beginning the work outlined yesterday by various groups, call for reports of plans, not only of work to be done, but for securing some of the necessary materials. Guide the Juniors so that different groups do not duplicate one another's efforts; help them to see how the plans of various groups may supplement and enrich what others in the department are doing. If any group is facing some problem as to how to begin or proceed, ask the group as a whole to make suggestions; do not make these yourself, but ask the kind of questions that will guide Junior thinking.

Work Period. This will proceed in the light of yesterday's planning and today's discussion preceding the work period.

Preparation for Worship. If there is time, call attention to the open Bible which has been made a part of the worship center. Recall what the Bible meant to Euplius. If a Bible in another language was used on the objects table yesterday, ask someone to bring it now, and lead the Juniors in a discussion of how the painstaking care of Bible translators has been a way of serving Jesus by spreading to many peoples the story of his life and death, and his message of God's love for the world. Ask the Juniors to choose a psalm or story of Jesus from the Bible which they would like to have read at the worship service. Call for a volunteer from the worship committee to find this and be ready to read it in the service which follows. (An assistant may need to help him to locate the story or psalm if he is a younger Junior.)

The Worship Service.

QUIET MUSIC.

CALL TO WORSHIP (chosen by the worship committee).

HYMN (about Jesus our Leader, or how we may show our love for him — chosen by the worship committee).

BIBLE READING *(by the volunteer member of the worship committee)*.

POEM: "Dear Lord, We Give Our Youth to Thee"[1] *(read by a member of the worship committee)*. (This is a suggestion only.)

> Dear Lord, we give our youth to Thee,
> In answer to Thy call,

[1] By Calvin W. Laufer. Copyright, 1927.

And pray our hearts may loyal be
To love Thee best of all.

Show us each day what we can do,
Where'er our paths may lead,
To dare the right, to seek the true,
To comfort those in need.

HYMN (chosen by the committee).

CLOSING PRAYER: Our Father, we are very earnest as we tell you that we want to be your dependable helpers. We know that you planned a good world for us to live in; that you put here all that men need to make them happy and strong, if they search for right ways of using their gifts and sharing with all. Help us to remember that your plan for a good world included us, the children. Make us thoughtful about finding out how we may serve with you, and make us eager to do our part. Amen.

SESSION 3. SONGS THAT HAVE HELPED US

THE TEACHER GETS READY

If the hymn, "All Glory, Laud, and Honor" does not appear in the hymnal your church uses, base your hymn study and discussion on some other familiar hymns, watching for the ideas in the words and phrases that will be richest in meaning for boys and girls. Explain all unfamiliar words to the group; for example, in Theodulph's hymn "laud" is probably the only unfamiliar word in the parts quoted in the story. Plan to send the Juniors to a dictionary, if you have one, or plan to explain this as praise usually given to God in our worship or hymn. The story will be useful to your unit purpose, whether or not this particular hymn is in your hymnal. Your pianist should be at the piano, ready to play as the discussion begins.

Be sure that the Juniors responsible for presenting "How Hymn Writers Have Served Jesus" understand that they are not to use this particular material in the earlier discussion but are to save it for the worship service as planned.

A SUGGESTED PROCEDURE

Group Study at Display Tables. Remember that the purpose of this is to discover the various ways Jesus' followers have found to work with him and to show their love for him. Encourage rotation at the various tables from day to day (not within the session). If any Juniors have brought additions for any of the display tables, these should be placed conspicuously, and the Junior contributor invited to explain his loan and its values for their work. Remind the Juniors at the various tables of plans made yesterday for the care and use of these Junior contributions.

Discussion. Ask someone again to give us the name of our new unit of work. What does it mean? Call for a brief résumé of various ways Jesus' followers have found to serve him, not forgetting the Juniors' report made day before yesterday of everyday followers whom they know are finding ways of being thoughtful followers. Notice especially any suggestions made about Junior ways of working with Jesus as his friends.

Ask someone to bring the church hymnal from the display table. Call on various volunteers for reports of ancient hymns: what they were like, what these hymns tell us about the writers and what they were trying to do, what makes these old hymns like or different from the hymns we like best today. Turn to "All Glory, Laud, and Honor"; call for a discussion of this hymn, using the questions on the board planned for the guidance of those studying hymns. If this hymn has not been previously studied at the display table, hold the hymn for use until after the story. Ask the groups to think of ways in which hymn writers have really been our helpers. Some Junior may be ready to illustrate his point with a special hymn that he may have in mind. If so, ask him to read this hymn if it is not wholly familiar to the group. If it is familiar, the Juniors might be asked to sing it together softly, thinking as they sing of what the hymn is trying to tell us or what the hymn writer was trying to share with us.

"Our story today is about a great and good man who lived more than a thousand years ago. It is his hymn that we shall be [have been] thinking about today."

Story. "A Song for the King" (see page 142).

Thinking It Through. "By what other ways did Theodulph

serve his Leader besides writing a song of praise about him? What are some tests of a real Christian?"

The second question should not be answered glibly. Offer the Juniors two minutes for quiet thinking in which there will be no discussion. Ask them if they would like paper and pencils for writing down some of the tests they have thought of. Younger Juniors who do not write easily may dictate their suggestions to one of the assistants, gathering with her in a small group for the purpose. The assistant should know that the only value of this work lies in recording the Juniors' own unprompted thinking. These papers should be put away until a later discussion.

As the Bible study today will take place in "Preparation for Worship," the Juniors may go immediately after the papers are collected to

Recess.

Work Period. Call for reports on the work materials brought in, and for what purpose these are planned. Present any materials provided by the school for this, and, if necessary, have the group make plans for their safekeeping and care. If this unit is being studied by an ongoing school, the supply committee will know what to do and will have the orange-crate cabinets or the regular closet for their safekeeping; a new school just beginning may need to make its own plans.

Continue with group work at the point it was left yesterday. Encourage necessary consultation and comparison between groups, but try to see that the Juniors feel responsible for a wise use of their working time, so that unnecessary interruptions are guarded against.

Preparation for Worship. See that all Juniors have Bibles, and ask them to find the book of The Psalms right in the middle.

"Why do you think the psalm writers wrote their songs?"

Call attention to the inscriptions of several psalms which name the occasions calling forth the song. For example, Psalm 55 gives the incident in David's life that inspired this song of praise for deliverance. Invite the Juniors to read the first three or four verses of the psalm as well as the last two verses. Psalms 54 and 56 are other songs of prayer and praise recalling God's care in times of danger.

Ask the Juniors to look at the psalms beginning with Psalms

120–134. If they have the King James Version, these are called "songs of degrees," but let them look in your Moffatt's Translation and read there what this means, or if you do not have Moffatt, explain that these are pilgrims' songs, sung as the pilgrims approached Jerusalem and the Temple to worship God on special occasions of joy and thanksgiving. The psalm the Juniors learned last week is "A Song of degrees." Let them find it. Suggest that they look at the beginning of several psalms to see what they can discover — Psalm 116, for example, in which the unknown writer merely tells of his wish to sing of his love for God. We do not know what happened that made him think of this, but we can be sure there is a story behind each psalm.

Ask the Juniors to think of events and happenings in our world today that make us want to offer a prayer or a song of thanksgiving to God. (It may be because things are not all fair and beautiful and we feel our need for God's help.) List some of these on the board as they are suggested, and tell the Juniors that we will continue our discussion beginning at this point tomorrow.

The Worship Service.

QUIET MUSIC.

CALL TO WORSHIP: A verse from one of the psalms, or something based on the New Testament (chosen by the worship committee).

(Example: *Leader:* Jesus said, "Come, follow me."
Juniors: His disciples made answer, "Lord, we would follow thee.")

BIBLE READING: Psalm 136:1–9.

READING: "Ever Faithful, Ever Sure" (*by a Junior,* who will explain that this song is based on Psalm 136).

> Let us with a gladsome mind
> Praise the Lord, for He is kind:
> For His mercies aye endure,
> Ever faithful, ever sure.
>
> He, with all-commanding might,
> Filled the new-made world with light:
> For His mercies aye endure,
> Ever faithful, ever sure.

All things living He doth feed;
His full hand supplies their need:
For His mercies aye endure,
Ever faithful, ever sure.

Let us, then, His praise sing forth,
His high majesty and worth:
For His mercies aye endure,
Ever faithful, ever sure.

HYMN: Hymn 23 in *Hymns for Junior Worship* (which was just read), or similar hymn of praise.

How HYMN WRITERS HAVE SERVED JESUS. (Two Juniors who worked at the Bible and hymnal table in Session 1 may read and explain an ancient hymn, other than " All Glory, Laud, and Honor "; the questions used for guiding discussion at the table in Session 1 will be of help. A third Junior may select a modern hymn of praise and read a verse or two explaining why he chose it.)

CLOSING PRAYER.

SESSION 4. PICTURES THAT MAKE US THINK

THE TEACHER GETS READY

Be alert to see that interest in the display tables does not lag. The Juniors have a real opportunity to think together about the many and widely different ways in which men have found opportunities to show their loyalty to Jesus, and their love for him and for others; this is the purpose of group conferences about the display tables this week.

The worship committee will need to meet with you for some help after school today in making use of group suggestions which will be given, in formulating the program for tomorrow, and in allocating responsibilities.

Try to have a Fra Angelico picture for use today in connection with the story.

Ask your pianist if she will play today a part of MacDowell's "To a Water-Lily" (see "Preparation for Worship" and "The Worship Service").

A SUGGESTED PROCEDURE

Group Study at Display Tables. Use the display tables again, rotating the Juniors so that all of them move on to new materials, new discussions, and new ideas. If any Juniors have brought additional materials for display, see that these are placed advantageously; call the attention of the assistant in charge of the table to these, and ask her to make particular use of them in discussion about the table.

Discussion. The Juniors might begin today by thinking of their own community and what they find is being done there to make people happier, healthier, and better able to understand what Jesus came to help men to be and to do. The work of the Church will, of course, be referred to in some way; but see that the Juniors become aware of other significant ways in which Christians make the message of Jesus real. Perhaps there is a specially friendly farmer or storekeeper who has done something for the Vacation Church School. There may be volunteer workers in the community who help there, or the Juniors may know of friendly neighbors who cheerfully run in to help where there is sickness or trouble. If some community-minded individual has given the town a library, or other gift for its enrichment, interpret this as the type of sharing that Jesus has asked of his followers who have wealth.

Call for several Juniors to bring pictures they like from the picture table, and to tell why they like them. Unless they have previously been helped to see real meaning in some of the earliest primitives, they will probably not choose one of these; choose such a picture yourself, and help boys and girls to understand what these pictures meant to people in a time when they could not read of Jesus, and had only the stories these pictures told to help them to know many parts of the story of Jesus. Explain, if this is necessary, how little artists knew in the time of the primitives (see Session 1, page 75) of the way to draw bodies or how to represent in a picture things that were distant and things that were near. They also thought that it was not respectful to show Jesus as a little baby, so they always showed him as a grown man, but very much smaller in stature if they wanted their picture to tell of his babyhood or childhood. Call attention to the rich ornamentation in many of these early pictures and how they included the high officers of the Church along with the shepherds and angels, and so forth, so that the people would know how very important these pictures of Jesus were to them and how truly beautiful they wanted to make them. The Juniors will have less difficulty in seeing real meaning and beauty in more modern pictures of Jesus; give them a chance to tell what they like about these themselves. They may want to read together one or two favorite Bible stories of Jesus illustrated by these pictures. Be ready to help them to locate these.

If possible have a Fra Angelico print on hand to show after telling the story which follows; either a Madonna or a picture of the transfiguration by Fra Angelico will be particularly appropriate (see picture list, page 184).

Story. " The Message a Paintbrush Told " (see page 146).

Thinking It Through. Show a picture painted by this artist and guide the Juniors to a real appreciation of the careful, reverent care shown in the drawing of the figures. Fra Angelico is noted for his wonderful colors and lines. Help the Juniors to understand what it must have meant to his brother monks to have these rare and lovely picture stories of Jesus and his life and work where they could see them every day.

If the Juniors ask about their test for a Christian, explain that the worship committee may wish to use this in tomorrow's worship. (See " Thinking It Through," page 86.) The committee will need the Juniors' further help in thinking about tomorrow's service. Let the Juniors use the rest of this time today in making suggestions to the worship committee for the service tomorrow. (See Session 4 of Unit I, for examples of what may be done.) Perhaps the group will want to take the unit title for the worship theme, and make use of some new discoveries that they have made about ways of being a good follower. (See also suggestions for worship for tomorrow's service, page 96.)

Recess.
Work Period.

Preparation for Worship. "Yesterday we were thinking about the old song writers whose songs have lived for us for hundreds and hundreds of years in our Bibles. Who were some of them? Why did they write their songs and prayers? [Ask someone to get a hymnal from the table and find some of the titles of the hymn tunes we use in our hymns. Perhaps your Juniors have never noticed these tune titles in smaller print under the hymn title.]

"The psalms were sung to special tunes also. Sometimes they were sung by great choirs of priests. Sometimes they were sung by the crowds of pilgrim worshipers. Sometimes they were sung by little family groups on the roof tops under the stars. Always the singers knew what tune went with each psalm. Would you like to know some of the tune titles and what they mean? Would you like to know how the music was played and sung? [Use your Moffatt's Translation of the Bible for this.]

"You will notice also that often the directions as to how the psalm is to be sung or played are given. The 'Chief Musician' referred to so often is the choirmaster who trained the priestly singers in God's worship. Look at Psalm 4. What does it say just above the author's name? What do you think 'Neginoth' means? [It is the accompaniment played on stringed instruments.] Look at Psalm 5. What are they to play this tune on? [Nehiloth, according to Moffatt, means, "Arranged for flutes."] Look at Psalm 6. On what will this tune be played? [Stringed instruments.] This psalm tells for what voices it is arranged. 'Sheminith' means that this tune is intended for bass voices. Psalm 9 is interesting. Upon what, or for what is it arranged? 'Muth-labben' says to the choirmaster, 'This tune must be sung by a soprano boys' choir.'

"Now let's look at the tune names which some psalms bear. Let's see what the tune of Psalm 22 is and what it means. [This is indicated in the marginal reading, though Moffatt translates "Aijeleth hash-Shahar" in our more everyday way of speaking, "Deer of the Dawn," rather than, "Hind of the Morning."]

"Did you know that there are love songs in the Bible too? Let's look at one [Psalm 45]. The choirmaster reads the tune 'Shoshanim' and knows that this is the tune known as 'The Lilies.' The theme of this song of love is in the second verse.

Do you want to read it? Do you know an American composer who called a tune of his 'To a Water-Lily'? [If possible have the pianist play a bit of this.] Much of the ancient psalm music has been lost, though some of it still lives and is used today. We know that the Jews of old wrote their most beautiful songs for the worship of God, and only their most skilled musicians were allowed to play in God's service."

The Worship Service.

QUIET MUSIC: MacDowell's "To a Water-Lily" if this is possible; if not, use " Kol Nidre " or another old tune from the church hymnal.

CALL TO WORSHIP:

Leader: " Blessed is the man that walketh not in the counsel of the wicked,
Nor standeth in the way of sinners,
Nor sitteth in the seat of scoffers."

Juniors: " But his delight is in the law of the Lord;
And on his law doth he meditate day and night."

All Together: " For the Lord knoweth the way of the righteous;
But the way of the wicked shall perish."

SONG: Song based on a psalm, such as " Ever Faithful, Ever Sure," sung yesterday (based on Psalm 136) ; " The Lord Is My Shepherd, No Want Shall I Know "; or " The King of Love."

PRESENTATION: How Writers Have Served God *(by two or three Juniors)*.

TALK *(by leader)*: Brief talk pointing out how it is through men's thought of God, and their experience with him, that the books that help us come to be. The idea of the value of taking time to think of God's wonderful work, his good gifts, and the many evidences of him that we all see about us in our world should be a part of this talk, but should not be merely the moral tacked on at the end.

HYMN (chosen by committee).

CLOSING PRAYER: Thanks for God's goodness and for men's opportunity to serve God through their best thoughts — thoughts that find their way into songs and poems and books of many kinds.

SESSION 5. FOLLOWERS OF JESUS

THE TEACHER GETS READY

Preparation will depend largely on what has been happening in your school this week. You will need to pull together the experiences of the week, and to help the Juniors to be critical of the work that they have begun. They will also need your help in planning for their ongoing work next week, looking forward to the final program which in Session 10 closes the school (unless you are working on a five-week schedule).

New committees must be chosen for the final work of the school (unless you are working on a five-week schedule). Give some thought to this and to the points that will need to be taken up in the planning period.

One step in preparation is to read very carefully the suggested procedure on pages 31, 48, Sessions 2 and 5, Unit I, which give in detail plans for just such a period as you will want for today. Of course, your group will probably not be completing orange-crate cabinets, but the same procedure and plan for evaluation of work will be useful. The suggestions include ways of helping Juniors to think in terms of group-made standards for the evaluation of their work.

Be sure that the worship committee is ready for its part in making today a really worth-while part of the life of the school.

A SUGGESTED PROCEDURE

Free Play. This may be carried on out of doors, or individual work indoors may be done, as preferred by the Juniors.

Evaluation of Work Under Way. For suggestions for this period see page 48, Session 5, Unit I.

Work Period. Carrying out into immediate use suggestions and plans made in the previous period. Note that there is no new story for today.

Recess.

Election of Committees for Next Week. Election should always be preceded with expressions of real appreciation of the good points in the work of committees being replaced. Also, suggestions for improving the work of committees may be made to incoming committees. This must always be objective, based on actual Junior experience in connection with help given or not given by the committees going out. These criticisms should never be personal; Juniors can be led to take real satisfaction in addressing their criticisms and appreciations to the work done or to improvements that need to be made.

Planning the Final Week of Work. Juniors need to work with a definite end result in mind. This goal should be one of their own making as far as this is possible. In evaluating work this morning, and putting group suggestions to use during the work period, they should be helped to gauge what time will be needed to complete this or that part of their work. Though a final program is suggested for use in Session 10, the Juniors will want to formulate their own plan in the light of the whole unit of work and of the various activities which have been part of it. This plan cannot be worked out in detail today, but the Juniors should be asked to think of various possibilities, and to come next Monday with definite suggestions for completing their work, and carrying out a final program.

Preparation for Worship. The Juniors may wish to take a minute or two to recall some of the interesting facts they have discovered about the psalms. Encourage the Juniors to think why the psalmists wrote these. Usually they wrote them as prayers, as thanksgiving for help received, or as general praise for the evidences they found of God's goodness in the world and in their own lives.

"How do you think the psalmist began his work when he wanted to write a psalm? What sort of things would he be remembering or thinking about? If you were going to write a psalm what sort of happenings are there in your world that make you think of God? What evidences can you see of his love and care of us? Is there anything about some of the people you know that makes you think that God is important to them? How does this affect us who know these people? Is there some way by which people far away, who cannot read our books or understand our language and songs, can still know God? Does it matter to us whether or not all people come to know Jesus and strive to follow him? Why? Are these things the sort of material out of which to build prayers and psalms? Why? Would you like to try to build one?"

Spend the rest of the period discussing with the Juniors which of these (or other suggestions that they may make) they would like to include in their psalm. Guide them to think about ways of wording each thought so that it will be as clear as possible. Help them to be critical in deciding whether or not the phrase or sentence says exactly what they mean, and whether or not it will say the same thing to others who have not heard our discussion. Do not try to complete the psalm today, but be sure that some assistant is keeping a list of all suggestions made by the Juniors for reference at the next session.

The Worship Service. This should be planned and carried out by the worship committee. The committee may wish to make some use of the test of a real Christian worked out by the Juniors earlier this week. They need to understand that selection from among these will need to be made. The session may include a consideration of the contribution made to us and to Christians of all times by artists, in much the same way in which we have considered the contributions of hymn, psalm, and book writers. If the members of the Junior committee wish to present some other kind of service as a part of their worship material, by all means encourage this. The questions used at the picture table in Session 1 will help them in their planning, if pictures are to be used.

SESSION 6. FOLLOWERS WHO WORKED FOR PEACE

THE TEACHER GETS READY

The Juniors should be planning and working with the clear understanding that this is the final week of school (unless yours is a five-week school). New things ought not to be undertaken unless they are very simple and can be completed within a day or two. Encourage Juniors as they complete their own work to find ways of working with other Juniors whose enterprises are still far from complete. Discovering what another is planning and how one may help him with his plans provides a real opportunity for Christian comradeship and helpfulness.

Do not hurry the Juniors in their work on the psalm in the "Preparation for Worship"; allow time for real thinking and for critical appraisal in the light of group purposes in working out their psalm.

If you have any books dealing with Christians at work for the good of all (see book list, page 182 for suggestions) try to enlist one or more older Juniors today to do some reading during the first work period and to report on this in the discussion that follows. Be prepared to talk with the Juniors about the work being done by some of your own denominational missionaries; notice that telling a story of a missionary is one of two story plans suggested. Keep in mind always that the purpose of this unit is the discovery of ways by which Christians may be loyal and useful followers of their Leader, Jesus.

A SUGGESTED PROCEDURE

Planning Period. Additional time for consultation, experimenting, and group criticism will be needed throughout this week if Session 10 is to be the final day of your school (see suggestions for Session 10, page 111). Some things that will need to be thought of are:

Kind of program and what parts it will contain, such as:
    Exhibits (what these are to be and how displayed)
    A possible dramatization
    Presentation of special gift to proper representative
Preparation of programs
Sending out of special invitation to parents, pastor, and other guests (especially if someone is to be on hand to receive the gift)
Will there be a worship service, and how shall we aid our worship committee with this?
What individual responsibilities will need to be assigned for the occasion, such as seating guests, explaining and showing exhibits to visitors, preparing exhibit tables, costumes for plays, and so forth?

A Work Period. This might be used for a critical examination of work with a view to what ought to be exhibited and how; preparation of tables by a trial arrangement; making of labels for exhibits chosen; making decisions as to what unfinished work might be possible for exhibit purposes, and how it will be completed. Actual work on any enterprise under way should also be carried forward by individual Juniors.

Informal Discussion. See that the Juniors are comfortably seated in an informal group (out of doors if possible). Call for a brief summing up of some ways by which Christians have been working to make this world a better and happier place. Discuss at this time what some of your own denominational missionaries are doing toward this end. What are some of the biggest jobs that still remain to be done? (The Juniors, if they come from homes where there are habitual contacts with church and church work, will probably think chiefly of further missionary work, or the duties and tasks connected with their church experience. Help them to think of the conquest of disease, the fight against poverty and want in our own and other lands, the work for world peace and unity, the local community chest, tuberculosis drive, and similar projects, as a part of that Christian service that began with Jesus' concern for people, with the training he gave his followers, and with his command to all his followers that they love and help one another always.)

" Last week we heard a story of a great painter who thought of his pictures as a service for his Master and for his brothers in the monastery. Do you remember how he prayed each time before he began a new picture, how he paused often in his work to think and to pray? Everywhere today there are Christians who try to make even their daily work as fine as possible, a service to their fellow men; it is their way of helping God to make this world a better and happier place in which to live. In a city in the East there is a great surgeon who never operates on a patient until he has first had a quiet time for prayer. He thinks of his work of healing and helping as Christian service, his way of following Jesus. On the boardwalk in Atlantic City there is a Christian druggist who thinks of his work of filling prescriptions and selling medicines as his way of serving his fellow men. He works so carefully and measures his drugs so accurately that doctors

FOLLOWERS WHO WORKED FOR PEACE

and patients have come to depend on him. This same druggist closes his soda fountain every Sunday, though he could make more money on that day than any other day in the week. He says, ' I will serve the sick on the Sabbath, but I will not use the Lord's Day to make money for myself from thoughtless people who use the day only for their own pleasure.' [Encourage the Juniors to think of other daily workers who make their daily work a real Christian service in the community in which they live. Christian parents and teachers are good examples which ought to be familiar to most Juniors.]

" In every country in the world there are Christian people who by their daily work and everyday lives show that they are followers of the Lord Jesus. Our story today is about a Christian in faraway Denmark who found a way of his own by which he might serve his Leader and his fellow men." (Or, use a story about one of your own denominational missionaries if you have secured the necessary information as was suggested on page 72.)

Story. " A Man Who Worked for Peace " (see page 149), or a missionary story.

Thinking It Through. " How may Peter Manniche's service for his Master find its way to many lands? What could it mean someday to have Peter Manniche's students working as good followers in many countries? How can these followers work for peace? Can a Junior work for peace? How? What is a good way to begin? " (Adapt these questions or substitute thought questions of your own if you used the missionary story.)

Recess.

Work Period. The Juniors should have definitely in mind the need to complete in three more days whatever they have started.

Preparation for Worship. Call attention to the suggestions for content of the psalm begun by the Juniors at the last session. Have these read aloud. " What kind of psalm will these ideas make? Shall it be a prayer psalm? Shall it be a psalm of thanksgiving, or a prayer for help, or both? Shall it be a praise psalm, calling attention to all God's goodness to us? Shall it tell God that we mean to be his dependable helpers? Shall the psalm be about one or many good things? "

As the Juniors think about this, they should consider critically the ideas listed on the board: " Do they all fit into the kind of psalm we are building? Do any need to be dropped? changed? Should there be additional ideas to complete the kind of psalm this is going to be? " (The Juniors need not be concerned with the beginning or ending of the psalm today, but only with the way the main thoughts develop one another into a well-rounded whole which says exactly what they want the psalm to say.)

Help the Juniors to think critically about the wording of their ideas. If they are not sure, suggest that they look through some of the Bible psalms to see how clearly and simply the psalmists of old wrote their thoughts. It is not necessary that the psalms be written in Biblical style, though this can be done if they wish. But first they must put their statements clearly and exactly right in their own language, which is far enough to go with wording today. Examples of possible psalm phraseology are as follows, and you will think of others:

A simple but definite prayer idea, Psalm 25:22. (What definite ideas for prayer have we suggested for our psalm?)

An example of thanksgiving to God and praise for his wonderful works, Psalm 77:1, 11-20.

A song of loving praise for God's care for an individual, Psalm 23.

After deciding the kind of psalm this is to be, and the final wording of each of its statements, the next step is to arrange the carefully worded statements in the best possible order. They should follow one another naturally; they may need connecting words to insure this. Complete this main body of the psalm today without thought of Biblical language, or of beginning or ending.

The Worship Service.
Quiet Music.
Opening Hymn (chosen by the new worship committee).
Talk: A leader is one whom others follow. That is why in our work together this summer we have thought of Jesus as our Leader, and we are proud to be his followers. One thing Jesus asked of his followers was that they in turn should try to be good leaders of others, so that more and more people might come to know Jesus, the Leader of leaders.

Of course a leader isn't always one who actually stands or runs in front of others. We have found that a man can be a good leader by encouraging and helping others as Paul did, though some thought that there was little a prisoner could do. Some men have been leaders by standing bravely for the right, by defending and protecting with their lives what is good, as Euplius and other early Christians did. Some men have been leaders by teaching men how to sing their joy and thanksgiving to God, how to express their love and faith and willingness to follow Jesus through beautiful songs and kindly service, as Theodulph did in the song he wrote for his king. Painters have given us wonderful pictures that make us think of Jesus and what he means to us. Pictures in color and stone were once the people's only way of really discovering what Jesus was like. Some men have been leaders by writing good books for others to read, books that help children to read the story of Jesus in simple language, or the Bible itself in another language so that the story will go far around the world; or they have written books that call our attention to the way God works with people and invites them to work with him; or they make beautiful books showing how wonderful is our world and opening our eyes so that we may see God's handiwork there. There are many, many ways of being followers of Jesus and leaders of men. Will you be thinking about this today and tomorrow?

Poem: " The Better Way "[1] (*read by a Junior boy*):

> " He serves his country best
> Who lives pure life and doeth righteous deed,
> And walks straight paths however others stray,
> And leaves his sons, as uttermost bequest,
> A stainless record which all men may read:
> This is the better way."

Closing Hymn: " Take My Life, and Let It Be."
Closing Prayer. (If possible, this should have been worded by the Junior committee.)

[1] From *Verses,* by Susan Coolidge. Used by permission of Little, Brown & Company, publishers.

SESSION 7. FOLLOWERS IN STRANGE PLACES

THE TEACHER GETS READY

Be sure that every Junior understands clearly the details of the final program planned by the group, and his own individual responsibility in seeing it through.

A SUGGESTED PROCEDURE

Planning Period. Today the Juniors should work out the details of their final program and review responsibilities assigned to individuals and to groups for seeing it through. The program and Juniors responsible for each part of it should be listed prominently for reference for the remainder of the week. Rehearsals should begin tomorrow for such parts as the welcome to visitors, explanation of the school's work and purposes, and explanation of pictures, if these are a part of the final program as planned. All speeches should be completely written and approved by the group today. Rehearsals of the dramatization (if some group has been working on one) and song practice should also begin today.

Work Period. For the writing of speeches, labeling of exhibits, preparing of invitations, and other details of the program. Juniors not needed for this should work on enterprises already under way. The dramatization might be rehearsed in this period also, in a corner behind screens, in order to get ready for presentation tomorrow for the group's suggestion or approval. The worship committee should complete final selection of hymns and the psalm to be read in final program. Close the work period by calling for a reading of all speeches, invitations, and labels. The group should offer criticisms for improvement and final wording.

Song Practice. On hymns to be used in the final program.

Discussion. "Yesterday we talked about some people who in their daily work and daily living find ways to be good followers.

FOLLOWERS IN STRANGE PLACES 103

Sometimes boys and girls let themselves think that this whole matter of working with Jesus is something that concerns grown-ups rather than themselves. Or perhaps they think they ought to wait until something really big or important happens before they bother to try to be loyal, forthright followers. Do you remember some things we said about boy and girl followers after our story yesterday? Do you think that we have found a way to do something worth-while for others as we plan for our final program this week? Can you explain your answer?"

Introduction to the Story-Report. "In faraway Germany there are boys and girls who are rather serious about this business of standing for what they think is right. It was not very easy to do over there in those trying days before the war. As you know, some Nazi leaders have persecuted some of their neighbors just because they are Jews or have Jewish relatives or ancestors. Any German who befriended them in any way was not only scorned but might even be severely punished for it by his Government. In spite of this, some German Christians have been determined that German kindness and justice shall not fail entirely in their homeland. A woman traveler in Germany tells us that even as war was beginning there were German children whom no amount of scolding or punishment by their Storm Troop leaders could force into unjust treatment of their Jewish schoolmates. Some of these boys and girls refused to play on a playground where Jewish children were forbidden to enter. In two different schools Miss Waln saw German boys and girls voluntarily choosing to sit on the hard, wooden benches reserved for Jewish children, sturdily facing the scorn of the other children and bearing the punishment ordered by the Nazis. Would you like to hear a report that Miss Waln makes of a German boy who was not afraid to stand alone in defense of those who were being treated unfairly?"

Reading Report. See "Jew and Gentile," on page 154.

Thinking It Through. "We are not often called upon to face punishment and imprisonment for being friendly to schoolmates of other nationalities than our own. As good followers of a good Leader, can we face bravely the teasing and laughter of comrades when there is someone who needs our friendliness?

How can we help the friendless newcomer or the unwelcome schoolmate? How can we help the unfriendly as well as the friendless?"

Recess.

Work Period.

Preparation for Worship. Call on one of the Juniors to read the main body of their psalm which was completed yesterday. Let another Junior remind the group again what kind of psalm it is that is being prepared. How shall we begin our psalm? (The Juniors will be helped by looking at some of the ways in which Bible psalms begin.) The examples which follow are selected more or less at random as there is no way of knowing what sort of psalm the Juniors have chosen to prepare:

For a psalm of love and trust: Psalm 18:1–3; 34:1–3; 40:1–4; 46:1–3; 73:1; 106:1; 116:1

For a psalm praising God's wonderful work: Psalm 19:1; 24:1, 2; 66:1, 2; 81:1; 92:1; 96:1–3

For a psalm which tells of our intention to work with God: Psalm 39:1; 41:1; 100:1, 2; 119:1–3, 33–36

For a prayer for forgiveness and help: Psalm 51:1; 64:1; 70:1; 86:1; 141:1–3

Choose the readings suggested for that type of psalm which is nearest to the one on which your Juniors are working and have them look up the beginnings of the psalm or psalm sections. (Do not try to read the examples for all four types.) The Juniors may adopt one of the psalm beginnings, or they may word one of their own, which would be even better.

"Next, how shall we close our psalm? Often the psalmists of the Bible closed their songs with a bit of good advice to those who wanted to stand for God among the people of their day. Perhaps you will want to close your psalm with a suggestion that Christians will want to remember and use." Look at the following for such examples and then let the Juniors word a final verse or statement for their own psalm.

Something for Juniors to remember and think about:

Psalm 27:14   Psalm 31:24

Sometimes the psalmist closed his song with a prayer, such as we find in:

Psalm 25:22   Psalm 19:14

Sometimes the psalm closed with a burst of song and thanksgiving, such as:

Psalm 13:6   Psalm 7:17

Sometimes the psalm ended with a declaration of trust in God or a promise to serve him:

Psalm 4:8   Psalm 29:11   Psalm 45:17

The Worship Service.

QUIET MUSIC.

OPENING HYMN OR CALL TO WORSHIP (planned by committee).

THE READING OF A PSALM (selected and read by a member of committee).

HYMN: "Take My Life, and Let It Be."

TALK: Ways in which followers of Jesus may serve him (*suggestions made by four Juniors*).

HYMN OR POEM (to be sung or read). (The theme should be working with Christ to make our world happier or better in some way.)

CLOSING PRAYER: We thank you, God, that you have made a place for us in your plan so that we can work with you in making this a good world. Help us to remember that we need not wait until we are grown up to begin our work for you, but that every day brings us some opportunity to offer friendly, loving service for others. Help us to remember that even a friendly word or an attempt to keep back an angry one can be a service for Jesus, our Leader. Amen.

SESSION 8. GOOD FOLLOWERS ARE NOT EASILY DISCOURAGED

THE TEACHER GETS READY

Today and tomorrow are our last working days; make your plans accordingly. Plan to help your Juniors to make the best possible use of the working periods today and tomorrow.

Note that the psalm which the Juniors have been working on should be finished today and ready for use in the final program. Will it be possible to make individual copies of this so that each Junior may have his own to take home after school is over?

A SUGGESTED PROCEDURE

Work Period. Any unfinished written work should be completed; group suggestions given yesterday should be used. This period may be used for whatever purpose the Juniors have in the light of their plans for a final program. Rehearsals, setting up of completed exhibits, song practice, review of a dramatization, or further work on unfinished projects all fit into the possibilities for this period.

Introduction to the Story. " One of the most difficult things that Christians must face comes when something is interfering with the good work they are trying to do. After France was invaded in 1940, there were hundreds and thousands of refugees who faced a homeless, heatless, foodless winter. There were Christians who were willing to help; the French people, themselves in great sorrow and need, still welcomed the refugees and shared with them as best they could, but soon there was little that they could do. A group of American Quakers, called Friends, went over to help, but they soon faced difficulties too. They could not get food from America through the blockade; there was a shortage of helpers and of money; there seemed to be no way to avail themselves of the help that America was willing to give. There was sickness among the families and all too few doctors who could be spared to help them. Parents had lost their children, and children could not find their parents. There were no ships and no money to send refugees to their friends in other lands. There were no houses in which to put them. You and I, had we been there, might have felt that we had the best of all possible excuses for giving up and just reporting, ' There is nothing we can do.' " (If you used the missionary emphasis day before yesterday, you may wish to develop this further today instead of using the material suggested here.)

Story. " Followers of Good Will," page 156. (Or use a second missionary story instead.)

Thinking It Through. When God planned our world he planned enough of everything for all his children's needs. To be sure he did not put enough of everything in any one place. He left it to us to share, to exchange, to give where it was needed. He never meant that each of us should live alone, with no thought for others, but his plans were so carefully and so beautifully made that we just have to depend on one another, have to make friends, have to plan and work together for the good of all. How do you think this world can really be the sort of world God planned? If it is to be a better, happier world than it is, how is it to be done? Who is to do it? Can we help? How?

Recess.

Work Period. Keep in mind that tomorrow is the last working day before the final program.

Preparation for Worship. Today the Juniors should complete their psalm. First they will want to read it through from beginning to end to see if it is clear and complete, just the way they wish it to be. If they wish to make it conform more closely to the Biblical language (and it cannot be overemphasized that this is not at all essential) this can be easily done. For the most part nothing more is necessary than changing the "you" and "your" to "thee" and "thou" and "thy" or "thine," and the second and third person verbs, e.g., from "do" to "doest" and "doeth," or from "love" to "lovest" and "loveth." The Juniors may also wish to think up a name or title for their psalm. Here is the psalm prepared by one group, called simply "The Juniors' Own Psalm":

O praise ye the Lord,
For he is good!
He healeth the sick;
He putteth into the minds of men and women to be missionaries;
He putteth into the minds of men and women to love the Lord.
I will love thee, O Lord, my Strength,
For thou art our Father and Guide;
For thou art kind to all peoples;
For thou helpest us when we are in distress.
God is our Shield and Defender and always will be;

He helpeth us in all kinds of ways;
He taketh care of us at night;
His love will be always the same.
O praise ye the Lord,
For he is good!

When the psalm is complete, the Juniors should decide how they want it to be used in the final program day after tomorrow. Shall someone read it, or learn and recite it? Ought the whole group to repeat it together, either from memory or from the board? Is there some way by which each Junior may have his own copy to take home after the school is over? These are questions for Junior decision.

The Worship Service.

QUIET MUSIC.

CALL TO WORSHIP:

Leader: " Bear ye one another's burdens, and so fulfil the law of Christ."

Juniors: " If thine enemy hunger, feed him; if he thirst, give him to drink."

All Together: " Inasmuch as ye did it unto one of these my brethren, even these least, ye did it unto me."

HYMN (chosen by worship committee).

BIBLE READING: I Corinthians 13:4–10 (*read by a Junior*).

SCRIPTURE (*read in unison*): Some memory psalm, perhaps the Twenty-third.

THE JUNIOR PSALM (*to be read by the group together*).

CLOSING HYMN (chosen by Junior committee).

CLOSING PRAYER (*offered by the leader*).

SESSION 9. WE TOO MAY SERVE

THE TEACHER GETS READY

Plan to make the final informal discussion period today an especially happy experience. It can so easily be spoiled by using it as a last opportunity to " preach at " the Juniors!

The room and supplies committees should see that everything is in order for work today. Plan to be on hand early to meet them.

A SUGGESTED PROCEDURE

Work Period. This will be needed for final tryouts on all speaking parts, for critical examination of exhibits as set up and labeled, and for completing final touches on all work under way. The period may need to be longer than usual.

Discussion. This is probably the last time your group can meet for quiet, informal discussion, and it might be well to help the Juniors to sum up some of the discoveries they have made as to what it means to be good followers of the Lord Jesus. See that the Juniors are doing their own thinking in connection with this, and not merely trying to guess what you would like to have them say. Help them to interpret the good work which they have done in their school as a kind of Christian service, if their purpose has been to make others happy. Any gift that they have made for others and the final program which will be shared with others are real services if done in a spirit that reflects their Leader.

" When our school is over, we shall find that we ourselves have grown in many ways; we shall know a little better the kind of living that Jesus meant when he said, ' Follow me.' We know a little more about how to get along with those with whom we live and work and play; we know how to value and appraise what is right and good and how to improve what is poorly planned or carried out; we have learned how to replace shoddy, poor planning with sound, good planning. We know a little more about the Leader we have, who invites us to work with him and to share in his companionship and love. We know now that always close at hand there is our Unseen Leader and Friend ready to share the good and the difficult times we know, ready to hear us when we call upon him, ready with his love and help at all times. We know that no day need pass without finding some way of serving our Leader by serving others cheerfully and wholeheartedly.

" Our last story today is about a group of Juniors who found one way of being good friends to someone who needed their friendship very much."

Story. " Friends at Neighborhood House " (see page 161).

Prayer. Our Father, we have had happy times in our school this summer. This is the last day we can spend alone together in work and play. Help us to make this an especially happy day. And tomorrow when we shall be planning and thinking about ways in which we can help our friends and parents to enjoy our final program, help us to remember that work well done is pleasing to you. We thank you for your love for us; help us always to share that love with others. We ask it in the name of Jesus Christ, our Leader and Friend. Amen.

Recess.

Final Work Period. The worship committee members will want this time to plan the worship service for today, with your help or that of an assistant. They will want perhaps to use the hymns and Scripture that will be used tomorrow as well as the Juniors' completed psalm. This will help the group to feel at home and familiar with the phases of the worship materials that will be used tomorrow.

Preparation for Worship. This period today should be used to sum up discoveries made by the Juniors in connection with what it means to be a follower of Jesus. The remainder of the period will be needed for planning in detail the worship parts of the special program for tomorrow. (See the suggested program on page 111.) The Juniors should feel a keen responsibility for this part of tomorrow's program; responsibility for taking part as indicated should be assigned or accepted by the Juniors themselves as an example of Christian service which they can render. Be sure that they know what points of the program involve individual preparation and presentation and which is group work, or both.

The Worship Service. This has been planned by the Junior worship committee, and should be carried out as planned.

SESSION 10. EACH IN HIS OWN WAY

THE TEACHER GETS READY

Plan to arrive early today — earlier than usual. The best possible preparation for today's session is a sense of serene confidence and expectation. You will find that it is highly contagious.

Talk quietly and individually with those Juniors who have special responsibilities, to be sure that nothing has been left undone and that it is quite clear what they are to do and when.

If there is time before the first visitors arrive, call the Juniors together for a quiet song. Lead them in brief prayer that will remind them that their program, and their part in carrying it through, is indeed a truly Christian service of sharing.

The program which follows should not begin until the guests are seated. The early comers should be turned over to Junior guides, who will explain the exhibit of school work. Junior ushers may seat the guests for the program which follows.

A SUGGESTED PROGRAM FOR THE LAST DAY OF SCHOOL

OPENING HYMN (chosen by the worship committee).

WELCOME TO OUR GUESTS (*by a Junior prepared to do this*).

EXPLANATION OF OUR SCHOOL WORK. (A Junior may outline briefly the units which have been part of the school program. He may tell what he wishes of the school purposes and what discoveries have been made by the Juniors as to what it means to be followers of the Lord Jesus. Additional Juniors may give résumés of two or three outstanding followers and what they have done.)

HYMN: "All Glory, Laud, and Honor" (*by the school*). (This may be accompanied by the briefly retold story of its author, by a Junior.)

SHOWING OF PICTURES OF JESUS (*by a Junior*). (This will include an explanation of the importance of the work of early and modern Christian artists and how they help us.)

BRIEF DRAMATIZATION OF A STORY OF A GOOD FOLLOWER (if this has been one of the activities of any group of Juniors during the school term).

PRESENTATION OF OUR GIFT (if one has been prepared for giving, such as jointed toys for some children's hospital or day nursery or the presentation of the offering money, with an explanation of its purpose).

READING OF A PSALM OF THANKSGIVING (to be chosen by the Junior worship committee).

READING OF THE JUNIORS' PSALM *(by the school)*.

CLOSING HYMN (chosen by the worship committee because it is familiar to both visitors and Juniors).

CLOSING PRAYER *(written by a Junior or group of Juniors, and led by a member of the worship committee)*.

The Story Section

"COME, FOLLOW ME"[1]

Nathanael stood quietly under the fig tree that flourished in his garden in Cana. The warm sun turned the green spread of the tree over his head into a canopy of gold. He felt the warmth on his face as he turned his eyes to the distant hills and remembered his God.

"God of my fathers," he prayed, "your people groan under a great burden and there is no one to help them. In their eyes I read sorrow and fear, and in their hearts is the great dread that you no longer remember them. Bless us and give us a new hope; let your love dwell among us that we may again sing the old songs and remember your promise to save us."

While he yet prayed, there came a sound of running feet in the garden. Startled, Nathanael looked up.

"Philip!" he cried in welcome.

"Nathanael, good friend!" answered the breathless runner. "I bring good news. We have found him of whom Moses and the prophets did write. We have found him whom God has promised to Israel!"

Nathanael's heart beat a little faster. "Who is he of whom you speak?"

"Who else but the Promised One?" answered Philip happily. "He has called me to follow him! I will never, never leave him." he added vigorously.

"His name, Philip? And where does he come from?" questioned Nathanael impatiently.

"He is Jesus of Nazareth, the son of Joseph," Philip answered softly.

"You are joking," replied Nathanael. "Who ever heard of greatness coming forth from Nazareth?"

---

[1] This story is based on the following Scripture passages: John 1:43-49; 2:1-10, 13-16; 4:4-14, 27-40; Luke 4:15, 28-31; 6:12-18.

"Only come and see him for yourself," answered Philip, simply. "Then you too will believe that this man is like no other in Israel."

So Nathanael, half hoping, half disbelieving, came with Philip along the road between Jerusalem and Cana. There he met Philip's new Friend. He heard Jesus inviting him as he had invited Philip, "Come, follow me."

Nathanael thought that the first thing Jesus would do would be to organize an army and march against the hated Romans, but it did not happen that way. He followed Jesus, not into battle, but into a little house in Cana where there was to be a wedding. The mother of Jesus was there, and seemed to be helping in the preparations, for she knew all that was going on. Jesus took time to stop off on his journey to Capernaum to join in the laughter and happiness of the bride and her bridegroom.

Nathanael marveled that God's Promised One would find time to bless a little bride and to mingle with the wedding guests. Indeed at one moment, when the parents of the maid were painfully embarrassed because their refreshments had given out, Jesus came to the rescue. Though he had once refused to use his power to turn stones into bread for himself, Jesus did not hesitate to turn water into the wedding wine which in that country was always served on such occasions. Nothing must mar the day for the bride.

"It is as though he could not bear to see anything cast a shadow over her happiness," whispered Nathanael to his friend Philip.

"It is always thus," answered Philip. "Jesus wants people to be happy; he is always telling them to rejoice and be of good cheer."

Nathanael had more to marvel over as he followed Jesus day after day. He found that though Jesus loved to bring laughter to people, he did not hesitate to speak sternly when he saw them doing cruel and selfish things, or when he saw them dishonoring God. Once Jesus drove some cheating merchants from the Temple, for they were making it hard for the poor people to worship God. Nathanael could not bear to look into the flashing eyes of his new Friend as he rebuked the cheaters and drove them away. Day by day Nathanael saw the poor and the sick, the wise and the ignorant, pressing about Jesus. They listened eagerly while he told them that God had not forgotten them, but that he loved them and had sent him to help them.

"I am your friend," Jesus said over and over.

"He has time for rich and poor alike," exclaimed Nathanael in wonder. "Truly, there is none like him in all Israel!"

Nathanael came more and more to believe this as he followed Jesus day after day. He saw the crowds pressing about him in the city and on the riverbank, begging for his help. He saw him sitting by a well, talking with a lonely, despised Samaritan woman. Even Jesus' followers would never have spoken to such a woman before they learned that Jesus would have them friendly to all. Nathanael stayed with Jesus for two whole days in a Samaritan city, listening as Jesus told the outcasts of the city, "God loves you and has sent me to tell you so." He marveled that he, a Jew, should stay in their city, for none knew better than Nathanael how the Jews hated the Samaritans. Yet God's Promised One was offering his love and friendship to all alike. Nathanael sat in a synagogue on the Sabbath and heard Jesus teaching rich and poor, sick and well, wise and foolish, that God is the Father of all, loving all, longing to help all people.

Nathanael noticed with surprise that things did not always go well for Jesus. "You might suppose that one so loving and kind would be welcome everywhere," he thought to himself. Yet although there was always a crowd about Jesus begging for his help, there were some people who hated him and longed to hurt him. It was a sad day when Nathanael saw Jesus driven with threats out of his old home, Nazareth, for he saw the sadness in Jesus' eyes when the people would not let him help them. Sometimes there were tired lines on his face — not because he was tired of helping, but because nothing was harder for him to bear than to have men turn away from him.

"He never thinks of himself," Nathanael said to one of the other followers. "He tramps from city to city, over hills and through valleys. He wades the freshets and often I have seen his feet cut with the sharp stones of the road. How can he do all that he does?"

"Perhaps," said John, "when we have been with him a little longer, and have learned more of the work that he has come to do, he will let us help him. I know it hampers him because he can be in only one place at a time, and always the villages are sending messages for him to come to them. Perhaps someday he will let us go for him and help these others."

One day, to the joy of Nathanael and the others, Jesus did call them close to him. He was on a hilltop where many others were gathered close, and from the crowd Jesus chose twelve helpers. " I need you," Jesus told them, " to help me in my work. Come and follow me, and I will teach you; you shall go forth to preach and teach and heal as you have seen me doing. I choose you Nathanael, and Philip; you James and John and Peter and Andrew; and you Levi and Thomas; and you and you and you and you," calling four others out of the crowd.

Gladly the twelve who had been thus chosen followed Jesus from that day forward, learning of him and preparing to be his faithful, dependable helpers. And in a little while, so well had they listened and watched and obeyed, Jesus found that he could trust them and use them in his great work of helping others. From that day to this the world has never forgotten the work of the Twelve, who all, save one, remained faithful and true to the end of their lives.

LEVI THE OUTCAST FINDS A NEW FRIEND [1]

On the north shore of Lake Galilee, just where the highway passed through the border from the territory of King Philip to the territory of Herod Antipas, stood the tax collector's booth. All day and every day this place was crowded with people. It was strange to pass through the crowd and listen to the many foreigners and strangers who talked together there while all awaited their turn to pay their taxes and tolls. There were humble fishermen passing with their day's catch, and ordinary travelers on their way to Caesarea Philippi. There were merchants from Egypt and Damascus who came this way hoping to sell their goods to the Roman nobles who dwelt in the lake towns. These had their wares unrolled and spread out for the eyes of the collector of customs, and many a shrill argument arose as to the amount of tax due.

[1] This story is based on Matthew 9:9–13.

The man who sat in the booth was Levi, a Jew who could both read and write with great ease. All day he was busy inspecting wares and merchandise, questioning the travelers, issuing receipts and making change, inscribing the record of the day's receipts on the great roll. He was used to disagreeable happenings — being yelled at by some hurrying merchant who thought him too slow, being scolded by someone who thought he had overcharged him, being scorned by his fellow countrymen, who hated taxgatherers. Levi went about his work carefully, exacting the last penny of toll even from his angrily protesting countrymen.

"To think that a Jew would turn publican!" Daily he heard the words of scorn pass from lip to lip.

Then came a day that Levi was never to forget. The morning was clear and bright, and many men were gathered about the customs booth. The babel of shouts and calls, the constant noise of many people talking in many languages had seemed a little worse than usual. Moreover Levi was conscious of the little knots of his scornful countrymen who waited to pay their tax and to be on their way, men who discussed him loudly as one who was a traitor to his own people. Levi did not see the sunlight that dappled the blue lake with silver, nor feel the soft breeze that should have cooled his flushed cheeks. He was too busy pretending to be deaf to the unfriendly voices all about him, and blind to everything except goods and money.

So when someone called, "Levi!" in a warm and friendly tone, the tax collector looked up startled. Who in all the length and breadth of the land would speak to him in such a kindly way? In a moment he found himself looking into the eyes of a Stranger, and there was something so friendly and welcoming in those eyes that Levi's hands unclenched and the silver coins he held dropped unheeded to the ground.

"Teacher," he cried wonderingly, "who are you?"

"Come and follow me, Levi, and you shall know," was the gentle answer.

And Levi obeyed! Right there and then Levi left the tax booth, with all its records, its money, and its waiting travelers, and followed after the Man who had spoken to him as a friend. Never had Levi felt toward any man what he felt toward this Man. The Stranger, he learned, was Jesus of Nazareth. He had no grand office to give Levi, no chance to make money. There was only the invitation to come and learn of him what it meant to live for others, rather than for oneself, and suddenly Levi found that he didn't want to be anywhere else.

Then one day very soon after Levi had found his new Friend, he did a very daring thing. He invited Jesus to his house to dinner. Would he come? Levi watched the face of his new Friend anxiously as he waited for his answer. Well he knew the storm of anger that the men of the town would loose on Jesus if he did accept, for no Jew in good standing would dare to be seen in the company of a taxgatherer, whom all men called a publican and a sinner. Perhaps — perhaps he should not have asked him.

But the same warm, friendly light was in the eyes of Jesus as he answered: " Of course I'll come, Levi. Count on me."

And, oh, what a feast it was that Levi prepared for his new Friend! The best of food, the choicest of meats and sweets, the highest place at the head of the feast were saved for Jesus. The men of the town were filled with anger as they saw Jesus turn into the house of Levi as into the house of a friend. More than that, they pointed with scorn as they saw that other publicans came gladly to the feast, happy to be near One who offered his friendship to all.

" How does your Master dare to eat with sinners? " they demanded of Jesus' followers, but it was Jesus who answered.

" You have many friends," he said, " but these have no other friend than me. A doctor doesn't call on those who are well; he goes only to help those who are sick and need his help. Levi needs me, and I need him."

The watching townsmen were surprised indeed at these words. Perhaps they thought that Jesus would change his mind when he learned how all men hated publicans, but Jesus did not change. Indeed, when he looked about him for the twelve best helpers he could find, Levi was one of those he called first to come and be one of his own disciples. Again Levi gladly obeyed and gave up forever his chance to make much money at the tax booth, for he counted the friendship of Jesus as his richest possession.

SOME STORIES PETER DID NOT TELL [1]

The old man sat by the window where the last glow of the sun touched his white hair with gold. On his knee was a parchment scroll which he had been reading with deep interest, but now the scroll lay unheeded. The old man's eyes were turned to the setting sun and there was a smile of peace that told of a heart that was well content.

Suddenly there was a knock at the door.

"Enter, my son," called the old man, and the door opened to admit a young scholar, who carried a second parchment. The young man approached the old man reverently.

"Master, it is I, your disciple Polycarp. I have been copying this section of the Word; it tells of the work of our Lord. I have been reading how he came from the mount of temptation and how he went to Galilee teaching and healing the many who came to him. Yet all this was after the death of your first master, John the Baptist, and much must have happened between our Lord's return from the mountain and the death of the baptizer. Surely there is more to know of our Lord and his work than appears in these few pages. You knew him well, and I would hear the story from your own lips."

The old man's eye fell on the parchment that lay on his own knee. "I too have been reading from the Word which Peter gave to Mark and which Mark has written down for the churches. I have been thinking of the very time of which you ask, for Peter has said nothing of all that happened after the baptizer pointed us to the Christ, and before Christ turned north into Galilee. And now only I, John, am left to tell of these things."

Polycarp settled himself on the long bench to listen as John continued: "I was remembering, as you came in, the day when Andrew and I stood near the city with our master, John the Baptist. Suddenly our master cried out to us, ' Behold, the Lamb of

---

[1] This story is based on John 1:35-42; 2:13-17. It is generally accepted by Biblical scholars that Mark's Gospel was largely inspired by Peter and was the first to be written. The incidents mentioned in this story are found only in a Gospel not inspired by Peter. Polycarp is also generally believed to have been one of the disciples of the Apostle John.

God!' There was such joy and reverence in his voice that we knew that there before us walked the Promised One, who had come at last, even Jesus of Nazareth. Andrew and I looked at each other and then, before we realized it, we had left the baptizer standing there and were hurrying after the Man who walked just ahead of us along the river road. As we followed after him, we were taken by surprise to see that the Man had stopped and was waiting for us.

"'What seek ye?' he asked quietly, as we almost stumbled against him. Our hearts trembled with fear, for we had been bold indeed to press so closely upon him.

"'Master,' we stammered, 'where — where abidest thou?' We scarcely dared to raise our eyes to his, and stood half expecting a sharp rebuke. But there was only kindness in his voice as he answered us, 'Come, and you shall see.'

"And then, Polycarp, the Master led us to the humble little house where he was staying in those days. Then, as now, the sun was dropping low in the skies, for it was about the tenth hour. He was so friendly and so kind that suddenly we lost all our fear and pressed him with our questions. Patiently he answered them all. Then he asked us about our work and about our homes; somehow we felt that he was seeing deep into us, knowing us better than we knew ourselves. We stayed with him until darkness fell; we were reluctant to leave him. Only the promise that we should see him and talk with him again made parting from him possible.

"We walked back to the city with our heads in the clouds, each thinking his own thoughts. When we said good night, Andrew added, 'I must search for Simon my brother, for I shall never be content until he knows our Rabbi as we know him.'"

"And is that how Simon came to know Jesus?" asked Polycarp.

"That is how it happened," John answered smiling. "Andrew could not rest until he had brought his brother to Jesus. Jesus gave Simon the name the Church knows and loves today. 'You are Simon,' Jesus said, when Andrew returned to him bringing his brother, 'but you shall be called Peter.'"

Eagerly Polycarp called forth other stories, stories of Philip and Nathanael, stories of Cana and the happenings there, stories of the trip down into the city where Jesus sternly drove the cheaters from the holy Temple. John told of many things that were not to be found on the parchment which Mark had written for the churches, things that were precious memories to John.

"I was a young man in those days," John added at last. "My muscles were strong but my heart was filled with passion and selfishness. As I think back I marvel that my Lord was so patient with me, for I was far from patient with others. James, my brother, and I loved him from the first and followed him gladly into the city, hearing how wisely he taught men of God, and seeing with our own eyes the wonders he did.

"There came a time when we knew that we must hasten back to Galilee, for our father needed our help with the fishing, and we had been long away. Jesus too was going north, and for a while our roads ran together. Only those who have walked and talked with the Master can know what it was like," added John dreamily, his thoughts far away from the room where Polycarp sat listening. "You will have to guess what that long walk with him meant to my brother and me, and to those who were in our company. At last we came to the place where our roads parted. The Master's road led west, for he was, I think, on his way to his home in Nazareth. Our road home led to the east. One thought comforted us — our Rabbi would surely come to the lake towns and someday we should find him again. Perhaps in the great work that he had to do he could use us, and we need never part from him again."

"And well I know that one day he did come to Capernaum by the Sea of Galilee and dwelt there among you all," declared Polycarp, glancing at the parchment he held. "It is all written here — how he called first the four of you, you and your brother James, and Andrew and his brother Simon, to leave your nets and come and follow him. You were his first chosen helpers."

"Nor have I ever left off following him, my son, nor will until I die," concluded the old man, peering at his pupil in the gathering darkness. "Now it is time for food and rest; another day I will tell you more of my Master, whom I love better than life."

And as Polycarp turned away he was thinking how the young fisherman John had grown through the years more and more like his Master, and how he had served him faithfully all the days of his life.

THE SONS OF THUNDER LEARN A NEW WAY[1]

Capernaum, the great lake city, was much excited over the new Teacher, Jesus of Nazareth. Every waking hour, and often far into the night, he was to be found teaching the townsmen.

"If you knew God better, you could not go so sad-eyed and heavyhearted about your work," he told them. "Just as you love your children, so your Father in heaven cares for you. God sent me to tell you so."

These were strange words to the people who lived by the lakeside. "Truly God sent him to us," they told one another, and the story of the new Teacher and his loving, helpful words and acts spread over the countryside. So days full of teaching and healing followed one another until people marveled at the strength of the new Teacher. He never faltered, no matter how much there was to do.

But Jesus had a plan. He had never forgotten the fishermen who had walked part way home with him. One day he left the pressing crowds in the city to walk along the lake shore. It was not long before he came upon Simon and his young brother Andrew casting their nets into the sea. He called to them, and was glad when he saw that they recognized him joyfully.

"Come and follow me," he called to them. "I need your help. I'll teach you to catch something more important than fish."

In their joy the two brothers beached their boat, leaving it just as it was, the wet nets still hanging over the side. They followed him. Jesus did not turn back into town, for he was looking for John and his brother too. He knew that in them too he would have obedient, loyal helpers.

Soon he came upon John and James. They were perched on the side of their father's overturned fishing boat mending their nets after the catch. Yet so glad were John and James to welcome the Teacher whom they loved that they ran to meet him joyously at his first call, leaving their father, the boat, and the nets.

At first these fishermen were not very much help. There was

---

[1] This story is based on Mark 1:16–20; 10:35–37; Luke 9:46–56; Acts 12:1–3.

so much that they needed to learn. Sometimes their very loyalty got them into difficulties. Each of them wanted to stay close to Jesus. Each hoped that when Jesus finally set up the new Kingdom he loved to talk over with them, he would be chosen to sit by the King. Sometimes Jesus was a little sad because he found it so hard to make them understand that in his Kingdom there would be no throne. His Kingdom was to be one of love, and his followers' chief service was to be love to God and to their fellow men.

One day after Jesus had chosen twelve helpers, he heard them quarreling about who should be greatest in his new Kingdom. He drew close a little child who had been trying to reach Jesus through the little company, and he put his arm about him. Then he looked up sternly at these quarreling men. "This child loves and trusts me though I have no crown or scepter," he told them. "He is happy just to be near me. In my Kingdom he that is content to be least important is most important to me."

Another day John came to Jesus looking very important. "Master," he cried like one who expects to be greatly praised, "we saw a man healing one insane as we came along. He was doing it in your name, but we told him to stop. He is not one of us who follow you."

Jesus looked at his disciple sorrowfully. "That was wrong, John," he said quietly. "That man was not against you. He was for you. One who can do such things in my name will not speak evil of me. You have driven away one who was on my side." It was about this time that Jesus began to call James and John the "sons of thunder" because of their stormy tempers.

There came a time when Jesus knew that he must face the hardest thing of all. He must go to Jerusalem where many enemies wanted only a chance to kill him. Yet he did not hesitate; he set his face steadfastly to go to Jerusalem. On the way south he sent some of his followers ahead to see if a certain little Samaritan village would let him stay there overnight on his journey. The journey through the Samaritan village would have shortened his travel considerably. Soon the disciples came hurrying back, their faces red with anger, their voices loud with protest.

"Master," cried John indignantly, "the Samaritans would not receive us, nor you. Have they forgotten all your kindness to them, how you once tarried with them in another town as their friend? Surely they need a good lesson! Let James and me ask God to send a fire to burn their wicked village and them!"

"O John, have you still not learned that this is not the way I would have my work done? I have come to save men, not to destroy them. Come, we will go by another way."

The sons of thunder as well as the other disciples met their hardest test when the time came for Jesus to leave them. They had not dreamed of such a thing. They did not want to talk about it. Perhaps it was because they had not been willing to listen that they failed to remember afterward that Jesus had promised that he would overcome death and would be with them always. They did not understand how this could be. So when they laid Jesus away one day in a rocky tomb they were dazed and blinded by grief. Even when friends came soon afterward to say that Jesus was not really dead but alive forevermore, that they had seen and spoken to him, the unhappy followers scarcely believed.

Then one day the fishermen saw Jesus with their own eyes, and felt again the old leap of gladness within them which they had felt when he called them from their fishing. Then they remembered all that he had said, all that he had tried to teach them about his Kingdom of love.

"Now we understand," they cried. "We must help our Lord to bring about a Kingdom of love on earth."

One and all the disciples set to work teaching, preaching, healing, and helping, just as Jesus had taught them to do. Some worked in the cities, some went out into the desert. Some sailed away in ships to carry the message that Jesus came to bring, for they were determined that in time the whole world should know it. When trouble came and evil men tried to stop their work for Jesus, they could not. Even when the king sent his soldiers to seize James and put him to death, James went with them willingly. Better to die for Jesus than to live without serving him! One by one the faithful followers carried on, and one by one they gave their lives for Jesus.

"The Kingdom of love will come when all men know and love the Lord Jesus as we know and love him," they encouraged one another. "We must let nothing stop us — neither unfairness nor lies, nor difficulties — no, not even death itself."

At last only John was left, but the young Christians smiled when he told them that once Jesus had called him and his brother the "sons of thunder." For none was more gentle and loving than John, now grown old in the service of his Master. Tenderly he taught the young, patient with mistakes as his Master had once been patient with him. For John had learned at last what Jesus meant when he spoke of his Kingdom.

WITH ONE ACCORD THEY CONTINUED STEADFAST [1]

In the upper room in the house of John Mark's mother a little band of Jesus' followers had gathered. There was Peter, who had loved his Master greatly but had suddenly grown frightened when Jesus had been taken prisoner. He had declared that night that Jesus was no friend of his. There too was John, to whom Jesus had turned on that terrible last day when he needed someone to look after his mother, Mary. There were James and Andrew and Nathanael and Philip and the other faithful disciples. They could not forget how once, in their fear and dismay, they had all forsaken Jesus and left him alone in the hands of the soldiers. Now each of them remembered with joy that Jesus was no longer dead, but that he had risen, and that he was still their wonderful Leader.

Some of them had talked with Jesus since that sad day when they forsook him; they knew that Jesus had forgiven them for letting fear get the better of their love. Best of all, they knew that Jesus had given them another chance to prove their love for him; he trusted them to carry on his work.

"We shall not serve him well by remembering how we failed him," Peter was saying. "None of you failed him as I did, and now no one will serve him more faithfully."

"We must not think of him as dead," added John. "For we have seen him and talked with him. We know that he is still our living Leader just as he was when we followed him all over Galilee."

[1] This story is based on Matthew 26:56b, 69–75; John, ch. 21; Acts 1:12–14; 2:14 to 4:24.

"Do you remember how brave and unafraid he was?" asked one of the disciples. "He knew that in Jerusalem men were waiting to put him to death. Yet he would not turn back."

"We begged him not to go," recalled another. "We warned him, but he had work to do for God, and he would not desert to seek safety for himself."

"Our Master was always steadfast!" Peter's voice was filled with love as he said the words.

"He will find us steadfast too!" they all promised.

That was not a very easy promise to make that day in the upper room. Only a handful of friends were there alone. Outside was the great city, filled with hundreds of people who didn't know or didn't care what had happened to Jesus; there were soldiers too who were determined to seek out and to punish all who had once followed after Jesus. Only a little while before, the men in this room had deserted Jesus and run away in fear. Would they really be braver now?

"It will not be easy," Peter reminded them. "We shall all face danger and some of us may lose our lives. Suppose we tell our Leader now that we love him and mean to be loyal to him whatever comes."

So the little company of friends bowed their heads. Each had things in his own heart that he wanted to tell his Lord. There was quietness and joy in that little hidden room. Jesus was there with them just as surely as he had been in the past when they had talked to him face to face. In the Bible, which tells the story of what happened in the upper room, we read, "These all with one accord continued stedfastly in prayer." When the time came for the little company to break up, each to go to his own room, they looked at one another with a new joy and a new confidence and went fearlessly into the dark city streets where danger awaited.

From that day on Peter found that his old fear had gone. He spoke boldly in the streets of the city and called upon all men to listen to the story he had to tell. And the story he told was of Jesus, how he had come from God to show men what God was like. He told of Jesus' life and death and how he arose from the dead and how he ever lives to be man's Helper and Friend.

Then Peter said the most dangerous words of all, the words that would make the rulers angrily demand his arrest. He said:

"We are witnesses of Jesus risen from the dead. We know that he conquered death for us all, for we have seen and spoken with him whom the soldiers put to death."

But nothing happened that day though Peter was ready to face imprisonment and even death if these should come. Instead, people looked up to him and said earnestly, "Tell us, what shall we do?"

"Turn to Jesus, and take him as your Leader, as we have done. Follow his way of love, and be baptized." And three thousand new friends joined the little company of loyal followers that day because of Peter's fearless words.

Another day things did not turn out quite so smoothly. Peter and John were going into the Temple for prayer. At the gate they found a lame man who had never walked. They prayed earnestly for him. Then Peter, in the name of Jesus, pulled the man to his feet and the man walked with them into the Temple! The people of course were astonished at what they had seen, but Peter said, "Our Leader, Jesus the Christ, can do greater things than you have seen." And he told again the story he loved best — the story of Jesus who can make weak men strong, not only strong in body but strong in spirit. This time, however, the Temple soldiers with their captain came and took Peter and John and put them in prison. During that long, dark night in prison Peter and John had much to think about. They were not worrying about what might happen to them; they were thinking about the many new friends that had been won for Jesus that day.

In the morning there was a tramp of marching feet before the door of their cell, and soldiers threw open the barred door and took hold of them and led them before the high priest. He had met with the rulers and elders to judge the two prisoners, perhaps to judge them worthy of death as Jesus had been judged a short time before.

"By what right, or in whose name, do you dare do these things, and say these things?" demanded the high priest sternly.

"By right of my love for my Lord," answered Peter boldly, "and in his name have I done what I have done. Will you condemn us for doing a good deed? The healed man is a witness to my Lord by his new ability to walk. Jesus, whom I will follow in life or death, is the same whom God raised from death."

The listeners marveled at the new Peter. The tale of his cowardly desertion of his Master must have traveled about the court, but anyone could see that something had changed the Peter whom they had known. They saw also the healed man standing in the midst, a silent witness for Peter and for the Master whom Peter now served so fearlessly.

"What shall we do with these men?" they asked one another privately. "It seems silly to put them to death for doing a good deed, and we cannot deny what we see."

"Let's threaten them that if they speak again in this name which they call upon we will kill them." And the council all agreed.

"We will let you go," said the high priest at last, trying to look kind, "if you will stop teaching in the name of Jesus. Indeed, you must not again speak in his name lest you die."

"Shall we listen to you rather than to God?" asked the man who had once run away in fear from these same judges. "We must tell what we have seen and heard." Nor could any further threats make them promise to be silent about Jesus. At last the rulers had to let the prisoners go. Too many people had seen the man cured in the name of Jesus.

So the two prisoners returned to their fellow workers and told all that had happened to them, and one and all lifted up their happy prayers of thanksgiving to the Lord whose name was above all names, and whose power could give strength and courage to all who called upon it.

SAUL BECOMES A FOLLOWER [1]

Saul the Pharisee was one of the busiest men in Jerusalem. Among the Jews there was none more earnest than he in the keeping of the law. In fact, Saul had little patience with anyone who failed to keep every rule and precept. Yet more than all he hated the little company of people who called themselves "followers of the Way." These followers were Jews like Saul himself, but they claimed as their Leader a strange, gentle sort of man called Jesus,

[1] This story is based on Acts 9:1-25.

whom the Romans had put to death. Saul simply could not understand how any good Jew could possibly look on such a one as Leader: yet this little company of followers were loyal even to death. Saul was determined to do away with them, unless they would give up their Leader and return to the ancient ways of his people. Many of the followers had been driven out of the city and into the northern cities of the land.

One day Saul went to the sanhedrin, made up of the seventy rulers who governed the religious life of Jerusalem.

"Give me letters of introduction to the Jewish rulers in Damascus," he said to them. "I have heard that in that city there are many followers of the Way who meet there in secret to worship their Leader. Let me search out these wicked men, and bring them back in chains, and you shall punish them."

So the sanhedrin gave Saul letters, and said to him, "Go for us, and bring back these followers of Jesus, and we will punish them indeed!"

Now it was about a hundred and fifty miles from Jerusalem to Damascus, and Saul, riding all the way, probably on horseback, had plenty of time in which to think. He was not able to forget how bravely some of the followers of the Way had faced imprisonment and even death for their Leader. Suddenly, as Saul rode along, a blinding light fell on him. In great pain and fear he fell from his horse. He could not see! He felt himself to be terribly alone. Where were his companions? Then came a Voice such as he had never heard:

"Saul, Saul, why are you persecuting me?"

Trembling with fear, Saul stammered, "Who — who are you, Lord?"

"I am Jesus, and it is I whom you would bind with your chains. It is I whom you would take back prisoner to Jerusalem."

Frightened and ashamed, Saul lay quiet, and the Voice went on, "But enter into the city, Saul, and it shall be told you what you must do."

Blindly Saul staggered to his feet; though the sun shone brightly over his head, he saw nothing. His companions took him by the hand and led him like a little child into the city. Poor Saul! He had planned to arrive like a big policeman, frightening men and women and children with his fierce scowls; but here he was, blind and helpless and frightened himself. He lay in a house on Straight Street where they had led him, too ill and blind to eat or drink. There was no one to talk to and, lonely beyond words, Saul could only pray.

Suddenly after three days there was a knock at Saul's door. A friendly voice called: "Brother Saul! Brother Saul!"

The blind man stumbled to the door and opened it. A cheerful voice said: "I am Ananias, a follower of the Way of Jesus. I have been sent to help you, Brother Saul." Saul felt a gentle hand take his.

"Why do you call me brother?" asked Saul wonderingly. "Do you not know I came to arrest such as you, to take you back to Jerusalem in chains?"

"Yes, these things I know, Brother Saul," answered Ananias, "and at first I feared to come, for all men fear you. But my Master has told me a wonderful thing. He told me that he had chosen you to carry his message to our own countrymen, to kings, and to all the nations of the world!"

Saul listened in wonder to the words of his new friend, and in his heart he felt a new happiness such as he had never known. Surely Jesus who had sent Ananias with such a message had forgiven him.

"I — I did not understand, Ananias," whispered Saul, weeping. "I never dreamed that your Leader would one day be mine also, that he would call me to follow him in the Way which you know and follow."

And Ananias was kind, knowing how shamed and sorry Saul was. He touched Saul's blind eyes and prayed for him; then Saul's eyes were opened and he could see the face of his new friend bending over him in great concern. He listened eagerly while Ananias told him all that he knew of Jesus, whose love was great enough to forgive even his enemies. In Saul's heart was born a great will to follow this Leader, Jesus, and to serve him all the rest of his life. From that day Saul was a different man.

Before long Saul had a chance to prove whether or not he could be a steadfast follower. The Jews at Damascus had been waiting in the synagogue for him to arrive and to call upon them. Each of the rulers was waiting eagerly to help Saul to arrest those who followed in the Way. When at last he did come to them there, imagine their astonishment when he said, "I have become one of them; I too am now a follower of the Lord Jesus."

They could not believe their ears. "Can this really be the man who drove many followers of the Way out of Jerusalem?" they demanded of one another. One and all they were angry at him and sought to kill him even as he had once sought to kill those who walked in the Way. They even set a watch upon the city gates lest he escape. But the followers of Jesus in Damascus stood by Saul loyally. By night they let him down over the city wall in a great basket, and so Saul escaped and lived to do a great work for his Leader. And none was more steadfast than he. Often his work brought him into great danger, caused him great suffering and weariness, but Saul was found loyal all the days of his life.

THE SON OF COMFORT [1]

The heart of Joseph the Levite was strangely light, considering that he was soon to become a man without money or property. He hurried along the sunlit streets of Jerusalem. As he ran a little breathlessly, his hand sought often the fat moneybag which swung from his girdle. It held the price of his little farm, which was all that he had owned in the world. He had sold it that very morning.

"It shall go into the common fund," Joseph said to himself. "How right and good it is that the followers of the Lord Jesus have decided to share all that they have with one another!"

In a few minutes more Joseph was thrusting the bag into the hand of the faithful Peter. "Take it," he begged. "It is for the brethren."

Peter's smile was very gentle as he took the bag. "May the Lord bless you, Joseph," he said. "You have given all that you have to your brethren, and yourself to his service. Once when I had pleased my Lord he gave me a new name, the name by which I am called today. Today you have pleased the Master mightily, and henceforth you shall be known by a new name. I name you 'Barnabas,' which means 'Son of Comfort,' for your gift will

[1] This story is based on Acts 4:36, 37; 9:26–29; 11:20–26; 15:25, 26.

bring comfort and courage to many a one in need." And from that day on Joseph was known among the brethren by his new name, Barnabas.

Day after day Barnabas served his Lord with gladness of heart. There was always someone who needed his help. Sometimes it was a man who was ill or in need. Joyfully Barnabas led such to Peter, and if he were found to be a worthy follower of the Lord Jesus, he shared and shared alike with all the others. Sometimes it was a new follower whom Barnabas saw wavering and discouraged. Quickly he went to him and filled him with courage and the comfort that friendliness always brings.

"How well Peter named him!" exclaimed the Lord's followers. "He is indeed a son of comfort to us all."

One day Barnabas sought out the brethren and found to his surprise that they were filled with dismay. It seemed that Saul the terrible was in the city. Every heart in that company was beating fast with dread. Everyone present knew how Saul, like a sword of the sanhedrin, was seeking out the Lord's followers to destroy them. Many of their number had already been killed or imprisoned. And now came the strange tale that this same Saul wanted to become one of their company, a follower of the Lord Jesus.

"It is a trick," cried one. "When he learns our secret meeting places, he will betray us."

"We must be wary," cautioned an old man. "It is not likely that Saul the terrible can change so quickly."

"Yet I have seen men changed in the twinkling of an eye when they came face to face with my Lord," said Levi softly. "Even so was my life changed when he said, 'Follow me.'"

Nevertheless there was fear and doubt in the hearts of the Lord's followers that day, for none could forget the cruel things Saul had done.

"But suppose," said Barnabas, who had been thinking deeply, "suppose that the Lord Jesus has changed the heart of this Saul as he changed your heart, Levi, or you, Peter. Would he not need our help? To whom else could he turn? Not to the sanhedrin, for if he refuses to harm us they will hate him even as they hate us. To whom could Saul go, if not to the followers of the Lord Jesus?"

THE STORY SECTION

But some were afraid to listen, and at last Barnabas left the frightened company, and went alone to think and to pray.

"Lord Jesus," he whispered, "if thou hast called Saul, then let me find him today and let me bring him into the joyous fellowship of thy followers."

And with the spirit of prayer still in his heart Barnabas sought for Saul; nor would he give up his search until he had found him, alone, discouraged, ashamed, and bitterly sorry for all the harm he had done.

"Why do you come?" Saul asked humbly. "It is true that the Lord Jesus has found me and has forgiven me for all the wrong I have done, but how shall I prove that I am indeed his follower if no one will trust me?" There was despair in the shame-filled eyes of Saul.

"Come, I will speak for you," answered Barnabas gently. "I am one of his followers, and I will be your friend. They will not fear you if I bring you in to them." And putting his arm about the bowed shoulders of Saul, Barnabas brought him to the disciples. Seeing, not Saul the terrible, but a humble, sorrowful man in need of their love and help, they took him in and welcomed him as one of themselves, a true follower of the Lord Jesus.

"Who is this man who sought me out in my loneliness and despair?" asked Saul, who could hardly yet believe in the wonderful thing that had happened to him.

"We call him Barnabas," said Peter.

"He is well named," replied Saul earnestly. "He was indeed a son of comfort and encouragement to me."

So it was that Barnabas and Saul became fast friends and fellow workers. Whenever there was something specially hard to be done in some city far from home, Barnabas and his new friend liked nothing better than to be sent out together to work out the problem. Wherever they went they won others to Christ through their own story of the happiness to be found in following Jesus. Saul, who was renamed Paul, was a brilliant man; he could make men listen when plain-spoken Barnabas could not. Soon people far and near began to hear of Paul's great power as a speaker; stories of the many he was winning for Jesus came pouring into the city. Soon people stopped thinking of Paul as Barnabas' helper and friend; they began to put Paul first. It was no longer

"Barnabas and Saul," but "Paul and Barnabas, his helper." But Barnabas did not mind. He was still much more interested in trying to be a real friend to those who needed him than he was in being first.

BARNABAS STANDS BY [1]

Barnabas, the missionary and friend of Paul, had a cousin who was called John Mark. This young man was probably very much interested in the stories his older cousin told of the various adventures that befell Paul and himself as they went about their work of serving their Lord. Perhaps it was because of his love for his cousin Barnabas that young John Mark decided that he too wanted to be a missionary.

Now Barnabas was very fond of John Mark. He knew how the young man had long dreamed of doing something important for his Lord. Barnabas did everything he could to help to make the dream come true. He even went to Paul, who had become the leader, and begged that his cousin be allowed to go with them on their first great missionary journey. Paul, loving Barnabas, consented, though he may have wondered what the young John Mark could do.

Perhaps Paul let his doubt show, or perhaps John Mark was still dreaming and so not quite ready for real work. At any rate, for some reason he did not measure up to all that he had meant to do. Indeed, right when the missionaries needed him most, he just said good-by and left them to get on as best they could. It was a great sorrow to Barnabas, but it made Paul angry. Paul never had much patience with anyone who let anything interfere with his work for the Master. He himself endured hardships with joy in his heart and never thought of turning back. But Barnabas couldn't forget the youth who had turned back.

"What John Mark needs is another chance," he told Paul, but Paul didn't think so.

"The Lord Jesus has a right to expect his followers to stand true to his work, even when danger and difficulty come," he said

[1] This story is based on Acts 12:25; 15:36–40.

sternly. "No, John Mark just isn't ready to serve the Lord with his whole heart."

"Perhaps now that he has had time to think it over, he will do better," pleaded Barnabas. "Perhaps he only needs a little encouragement from us; perhaps he just needs to feel that he is trusted."

But Paul would not listen; he would accept no second best in Christ's service. Barnabas, on the other hand, knew from experience how second best can become first best when love and trust point the way.

"Paul," he said simply, "both you and I love the Lord Jesus with all our hearts, but we serve him in different ways. I am not eloquent as you are. I cannot hold great audiences spellbound with my words. But I can help a man here or there by being his friend; that is my best way of serving my Lord. Paul, I must stand by John Mark. Who knows but he may someday become a greater missionary than I?"

Paul stood stern and still; there was a great, swelling pain in his heart, for he loved Barnabas, but Paul was sure that this time he was making a mistake.

"Barnabas, if you put John Mark before the Lord's work, then I must work on without you, for I cannot consent to taking your cousin with us another time. Our missionary work demands that every worker stand by with a loyalty that never wavers."

"Friend Paul, you do not understand. John Mark *is* the Lord's work to me, just as once you were his work for me. I cannot leave the youth alone and uncomforted. Perhaps God has different things for us to do, Paul. Perhaps he needs you to win the crowds that would never listen to me; perhaps he needs me to encourage and befriend a few people who might otherwise be overlooked or forgotten. We can each do our best for our Master in whatever service he asks of us. Good-by, Friend Paul, we part friends in a fellowship of love and service for others that will someday reach round the world. God go with you."

"And with you, Barnabas," answered Paul gently. And so the two parted, each to serve the Lord in the way in which he served best. Long after, Paul heard from a traveler how Barnabas and John Mark had made a new beginning, and had sailed away together to serve the Lord on the Island of Cyprus.

"The son of encouragement has won still another to the service of the Lord," he murmured, and in his heart Paul was glad.

A PRISONER FINDS A WAY TO HELP [1]

Paul was old and tired. He had served his Leader faithfully, yet here he was, peering through the dimness of a Roman prison, listening at every movement to the rattle of the chains that bound him. Who could blame him if he felt alone and deserted by the Master he had served so well?

But such a thought had never entered Paul's mind. He looked over at the young man Titus, his loyal helper, who was standing by him now in the dreary prison. Often Paul had said to this young man, and to other Christians who found it none too easy to follow their Master, "Quit you like men, be strong." Well, Paul was a man who could take his own advice. After all, his Leader had never promised his followers that they would find it easy to serve him. Indeed, he had warned them that there would be many hard things to bear. Their comfort and help was their sureness that their Unseen Leader would never, never desert them.

In prison day seemed like night and night was little darker than day. It gave Paul time to think and plan. Before winter, he was sure, they would come for him to put him to death, but he was not thinking of himself. What would happen to those new Christians he must leave behind? Would the older men and women face with courage the dangers that lay ahead, or would they shrink and turn away from their Leader when threats of imprisonment and death faced them? Was there anything Paul could do now to help them? If he had asked the Roman guard who stood near, a scornful laugh would have been his only answer. What could Paul, a tired old man, bound about with chains and under sentence of death, do to help anyone? But Paul had thought of a way.

"Titus, my son, I do not need you here any longer. You must go to Dalmatia to strengthen the brethren there. Tell them that I am not afraid but, rather, rejoice that so soon I shall be with my Lord, and that they must hold fast to Christ. But before you

[1] This story is based on II Tim. 1:1, 2, 8; 2:3, 15; 4:6–13, 21, 22.

go leave near me my parchments and pen for I must strengthen Timothy also. I would write to him to come to me and bring Mark for a last hour of counsel, for it is you young men who must keep faith with the new churches."

The young man Titus was filled with dismay at the thought of leaving Paul. Demas, the unfaithful friend, had already forsaken him in his prison. Crescens, who would have stayed to comfort the prisoner, had been sent away by Paul to carry help to the sorely troubled churches in Galatia. Tychicus had also hurried away to deliver a letter from Paul to the church at Ephesus. Only Luke, the physician, was there to stand by Paul. Titus wanted to stay too.

"No, no, my son," Paul shook his head. "If I could go myself to these sorely troubled Christians, I would, but I am chained. You must be my hands and feet. You must be my tongue and say the words that will keep love and courage burning high in the churches. I give you freely, though it is hard to part from you."

So Titus embraced the old man, and turned away to hide his tears. He knew that he would not see him again.

After Titus had gone, Paul, perhaps with the help of Luke, wrote his last letter to Timothy. Ah, Timothy was a faithful lad! Never once had Paul asked him to do a hard thing but Timothy had responded with all his heart. It would be good to see him again if only there were time. But perhaps Timothy would not get the letter in time. No matter! The important thing after all was that Timothy should be himself encouraged to be a good soldier of the Lord Jesus Christ.

Paul took the pen and in the dim light he smoothed out the parchment. What should he say to Timothy that would help him? Timothy had always looked to Paul for direction and counsel. Would Timothy be able to carry on a great work for the Lord Jesus if Paul were not there to help?

"He must! He must!" thought Paul, and in his heart he offered a prayer for Timothy and for the other young men whom he was leaving in charge of a great work. "What shall I say to Timothy, that he may never forget to be true to his Leader?"

Paul thought and thought; then suddenly he began to write. His trembling old hand wavered over the parchment, for he could scarcely see the words he wrote.

"Paul to Timothy, my dearly beloved son," he began. "I remember you in my prayers night and day. I greatly desire to see you, and the remembrance of your faith and your service is my comfort."

Paul paused. Would Timothy hold fast to Christ? Many Christians could not bear it when their neighbors laughed at them scornfully. Perhaps they were laughing at Timothy now on Paul's account! He could almost hear them saying, "A great God is yours when he lets his followers be put in prison! If he is so great, why does he not save Paul? Why does he not keep trouble and danger away from you Christians?"

"Be not ashamed of our Lord," Paul wrote, "nor of me his prisoner. Remember that he has called us with a holy calling, and he has a plan and a purpose for us. Hold fast to him, Timothy, and to the words of counsel I have given you in times past."

Paul's pen was still. Timothy was so young! He was not very well. He was a little timid when he had to speak to such learned pagans as the Corinthians. Would he be able to stand alone when Paul was no longer there to lean on? The pen moved on.

"'Be strong in the Lord,' my son. He will stand by you as even I never could. Remember that our Leader is looking to you to teach other men of him. So shall the word of our Master spread if you are faithful. Endure hardness as a good soldier of Jesus Christ. Study to show yourself approved unto God, a workman who needeth not to be ashamed.

"If so be that this letter does not reach you until I have gone home, you know well what I have taught, how I have lived, my purpose, my faith, my long-suffering, my love, and my patience. Continue in the things you have learned of me. The time of my departure is at hand, but watch in all things, do the work of a minister, make full proof of your love for the Lord Jesus."

It was so dark now that Paul could scarcely see the parchment before him. There was a dank coldness in the prison and his old bones shivered. Yet one thing more he must write, now that he had done his best to insure Timothy against discouragement and fear. He must urge him to come and see him if he could, for Paul longed beyond words for the sight of the youth he so loved.

"If you can, my son," he wrote with trembling hand, "try to come quickly. Only Luke is here, and I am lonely for you. Bring

Mark with you; he has turned out to be such a loyal helper. And bring my cloak that I left at Troas in the house of Carpus, and if you can carry them, bring me my books also, especially my parchments. Try to come before winter, and the Lord Jesus strengthen your heart in all things."

Whether or not Timothy reached Paul before he had gone to be with his Master we do not know. We only know that Paul went bravely, even joyously, to meet his Lord and that Timothy served the Lord faithfully and well all the days of his life. Timothy gave his beautiful letter from Paul to those who collected his letters for us, and someday you can read it in your Bible for yourself.

A COSTLY GIFT IS OUR BIBLE

The cruel emperor Diocletian was very angry. He did not like Christians. Indeed he had done everything he could to get rid of them. If an emperor wished he could order anyone to be put to death and it was as good as done. Because this was true, Diocletian was puzzled indeed.

"I do not understand it," he declared. "My orders are that all my people must worship me as their god. I have ordered that all who would not obey should be arrested and put to death. Yet these Christians do not bow down to me. My soldiers have arrested many of them and have put them to death. Yet you say the number of Christians in my empire is larger than ever." The emperor glared at his trembling minister as he spoke.

"If you will but listen to me, O Emperor," began the minister again, "I will tell you how to get rid of them."

"Speak!" the emperor commanded imperiously.

"Destroy their places of worship, so that they cannot meet together," whispered the minister craftily. "In meeting they cleave together and are the stronger, and new members are won by their courage and fortitude. But if there is no way for them to meet, they will not grow."

So the emperor ordered that every Christian church and meeting place should be torn down or burned with fire. Days and weeks passed, and still there were quiet, serene-faced people who walked the streets of Rome without bowing to the emperor's image. By tens and hundreds they were arrested, but still there were more and more. The emperor was angrier than ever, and sent for his minister.

"I have followed your advice," he declared furiously. "The churches have all been destroyed, but these Christians meet in one another's homes. They gather in caves and outside the city walls to worship their Christ. There are more Christians than ever!"

The minister trembled before the great emperor's anger, but he had been learning some things himself.

"Master," he begged, "they are strong because of a sacred book they own which they call the Scriptures. It tells of their God and of his will for his people. The Christians meet in secret to read its pages, and it makes them the more determined to hold fast to their Christ. If we could destroy the Book, so that not a copy of it were left —"

"Destroy them all, every one," commanded the emperor, scarcely waiting for his minister to finish. "We shall see whether the Christians shall continue to live and defy me. Kill every Christian who possesses a copy of this Book."

So the soldiers went throughout the land, searching the meeting places of the Christians and collecting copies of the Scriptures. The Scriptures in those days were not a printed book; every copy had to be written by hand, and each book was separate. People went to the church to hear the books read. Of course, these handwritten books were very large, and it was hard to find a place where they could be hidden from the soldiers. When the people heard that the soldiers had discovered the meeting place and were coming to search it, they would hurry there, and brave men and women would take one book or another to hide in their own homes. They knew that the soldiers would not be likely to search there for such a book, because few were known to be wealthy enough to have a copy in their homes. The soldiers' search was often in vain. They knew that the Christians had hidden the writings well.

But some members of the Church were not steadfast. They had seen how cruelly the soldiers treated Christians who refused to worship the emperor. So some decided to be on the safe side and made friends with the soldiers. They told the soldiers where the Scriptures were kept in hiding in the homes of the steadfast Christians.

The home of Euplius, one of these Christians, was searched. There the soldiers found what they were looking for. They ordered that his home be torn down, and that Euplius be arrested and brought before the governor.

When the governor saw this young man standing fearlessly before him, he wondered why he was willing to suffer for his religion. What was there in this religion that made the Christians willing to die for it? He decided to ask Euplius some questions.

"Do you not know that the emperor has ordered that all those who have copies of these writings are to be put to death?" he asked.

"I have heard of the emperor's orders," Euplius answered quietly and in a firm voice.

"Then why did you not turn over all the writings to the soldiers to be burned and save yourself trouble?" the governor went on.

"It it better that I be burned than that the Scriptures be burned," Euplius replied bravely.

This surprised the governor. He became curious to know what was in the Book that this young man thought was more valuable than his own life.

"Read to me from your Book," he commanded.

Then Euplius took the writings reverently in his hands. He turned the leaves and then read in a clear, ringing voice so that everyone could hear, "'Blessed are they that have been persecuted for righteousness' sake: for theirs is the kingdom of heaven.'"

The governor was furious when he heard this. He ordered that the cruelest tortures be inflicted upon Euplius. The soldiers did to him the most painful things that they knew. After each torture the governor called out, "Will you give up the rest of your Books to be burned and save yourself?"

Each time Euplius answered, "I will never save my life by burning the Word of God."

At last the governor knew that he was beaten. In great anger he ordered his soldiers to put Euplius to death, for nothing that he could do to the youth, he knew, would make him give up the

Book to be burned. Bravely Euplius went to meet the soldiers, glad in his heart that he had proved true to his Christ and had saved the Book from burning. Someday someone would find it and find strength and hope in its pages as he had. His last words were a prayer of joyous thanksgiving to his Lord that he had made him strong to face death for Christ his Leader.

It is because of Christians like Euplius that our Bible has come down to us through the ages. Over and over again wicked men have tried to stamp it out, to kill men for possessing a copy. At the risk of their lives men have cherished this Book. Women, knowing that the house was to be searched for it, hid it in the bread dough and baked it in the loaves so that it could not be found. Prisoners hid it in their pillows, and sent it out to the world page by page, as they could find courageous visitors willing to take the risk. Some died without wavering rather than betray the hiding place of God's Word. The Bibles that we hold in our hands today were given to us by these brave Christians of another day and age who were willing to die rather than have the world lose this precious Book.

A SONG FOR THE KING

The prisoner Theodulph pressed close to the slitlike window in the thick wall of his cell. His drab prison garments could not dim the joyous light that shone forth from his eyes. His bare feet pressed the cold stone floor and did not feel the chill. On his knee was a thin strip of papyrus, and on it Theodulph wrote rapidly. Now and then the quill paused and he gazed unseeing at the damp stones that hemmed him in. It was as though he saw beyond them the wide sunny fields of France, where birds poured forth their daylong song of praise; or perhaps he saw the great cathedral where once he had stood in rich robes of crimson and gold before the high altar, the honored bishop of Orleans. As he gazed far away beyond his prison wall, the good bishop hummed to himself the words he had written on his papyrus:

"All glory, laud, and honor
To Thee, Redeemer, King,

> To whom the lips of children
> Made sweet hosannas ring."

There was a rattle of keys and his cell door was flung open. It was the jailer with his supper, bread and a bit of cheese and a jug of water.

"How can you sing, sir?" he asked pityingly. "You, the great bishop, unjustly imprisoned here!" The jailer looked at the ragged prison garment and around at the bare little cell, with its plank bed and single stool.

"Better can an innocent man sing in his prison than a guilty soul that dwells in a palace," smiled the good bishop. "I have done no wrong and these stone walls do not come between my Lord and me."

> "Thou didst accept their praises;
> Accept the prayers we bring,
> Who in all good delightest,
> Thou good and gracious King."

"Can God be good and gracious who leaves you suffering here?" asked the jailer wondering. "How can you sing his praises, you who suffer so unjustly?"

"My Lord has not left me here," answered the prisoner simply. "He is here with me, Simon. And tomorrow when my boys come they will join with me in this new song of praise to him."

Long after the jailer had gone, the bishop bent over his song, changing a word here, a note there, until it was as perfect as he could make it. When the light was gone, he went happily to his narrow bed and lay down to sleep. There was nothing more that he could do that day; his song was done. Tomorrow the boy choir, which he had once trained in procession in the wide aisles of the cathedral, would stand in the prison yard under his window to learn the new song of praise, a song that would gladden the hearts of the people of Orleans.

"What does it matter," murmured the prisoner sleepily, "whether my boys sing the Master's praise in a lofty cathedral or in a barren prison court? My Lord can hear as well in either place," and with that he dropped into sound slumber.

It was a strange sight the next day to see the group of boys, both big and small, standing with upturned faces in the prison court under the prisoner's cell. Through the tiny, barred window they could scarcely see the good bishop's face, but there was not a boy there whose heart did not leap at the sound of his voice.

"A new song I bring you today, lads," called the bishop, "a song of praise that sang its way into my heart. Thus it goes." And the strong, clear voice of the prisoner spilled gladness and hope and love into the prison court until every boy there had been touched by it. One by one they caught up the joy of the song, until at the end boys and bishop were singing together as happily as though no prison wall separated them. The hour went by on wings as the song rose again and again, reaching every prisoner with its gladness.

"Come again tomorrow, my lads," called the bishop, when the hour was gone. "Soon comes the holy day when even the king will go to the church to pray. You must sing to him this song of joy as he passes. Our king carries a great burden; perhaps our song will make him forget it for a little while."

The boys below looked at one another in speechless amazement. Soon, indeed, the city would troop to the church to receive the blessed palms and to hear read the story of Christ's entry into Jerusalem, but the king was the enemy of their good bishop. Had he not cast him into prison unjustly? Why should the bishop care about the burdens of his enemy?

"But the king hates you," protested one boy impatiently. "Why should we sing for him?"

"Perhaps in his heart he really believes that I have wronged him," the bishop answered. "Who can blame him for that when I cannot prove otherwise?"

"But your people have told him over and over that you mean only good to him and the kingdom," declared another lad.

"Then let's prove it to him by lifting his heart through the joy of our song," smiled the bishop. "Let him hear us sing of the love of our Lord for his people. Perhaps he will be moved to praise his goodness with us."

It was a hard thing that the bishop had asked his boys to do. One and all they loved him; one and all they had suffered with him during his unjust imprisonment. Nevertheless they came each day to the prison court and lifted their voices with the bishop's until the beautiful song had been perfectly mastered, fit to share with a king.

At last came the great day. The sun poured down on the street thronged with the people of Angers on their way to church. Brightest and most colorful of the whole procession were the king and his attendants, dressed in royal robes and decked with jewels and chains of gold. Suddenly the king drew his horse up sharply. What was this?

Down the street came a procession of white-robed boys, their voices mounting as one in a song of wondrous beauty. They surrounded the king, with friendly gesture, and sang so joyously, so sweetly, that the king's eyes were filled with tears. Somehow as they sang the king of the land felt himself growing humble at the thought of a greater King whose subject he was.

> "All glory, laud, and honor
> To Thee, Redeemer, King,"

sang the boys, and the king and the crowd listened in silence. The king's head was bowed, and his people, watching, knew that he prayed.

"Who are you, lads?" he asked at last.

"We are the choirboys of Theodulph," answered the biggest boy. "He has not ceased to train us, even from his prison cell. He wrote the hymn for us."

"Who befriends the boys of the kingdom like that will surely do no wrong to the king," declared the ruler. "Tell Theodulph that he is free."

"Free! Free!" echoed the people, and the sound rang like a song down every street and lane, passing from lip to lip until the bishop in his prison heard it and bowed his head in a prayer of thanksgiving.

The song that Theodulph wrote nearly twelve hundred years ago is still sung wherever Christians gather. While the story of the bishop winning his freedom through its sweetness is a legend, the fact that he wrote the song in prison is known to be true. Refusing to let injustice make him bitter, he thought only of the good that he had known. He put his gratitude into a hymn of thanksgiving for the boy choir he had loved and trained even from his prison.

THE MESSAGE A PAINTBRUSH TOLD

The monks of San Marco crept quietly about the halls of the barren monastery. When they spoke at all it was in whispers. But in the eyes of every brother there was a happy expectancy. Now and then one of the company would climb soundlessly to the upper corridor to watch from behind a pillar the quiet figure in monk's robe at work with palette and paintbrush. Now and then the brush was still and the dark head of the painter was bowed in prayer. Always the watcher returned unseen and unheard to report to his waiting brothers.

" Brother Giovanni has begun a new picture this day," declared the watcher. " It is so beautiful it takes the breath."

" To think he came to us as a little clerk, who used his odd moments to adorn the tablets and walls in divers places in the town where he lived! Now he paints only for us." It was the jolly, fat monk who spoke.

" Brother Giovanni will cover the thirty-two panels of the upper corridor with scenes from our Saviour's life," added a quiet monk who sat against the wall. " He paints that we, his brothers, may remember Jesus' love for all men."

" Always he prays as he works," whispered a young brother but lately come to the monastery. " Nor will he begin a new painting except after long fasting and prayer."

" That is because he works for the glory of God," explained the oldest monk, who had just entered the room. " He works as though the divine Master moves his brush; and once having painted, he changes nothing."

" I would that God were as real to me! " sighed the brother who was oftenest in trouble.

" God has been nearer to me since Giovanni began his work among us," declared the monk whose tired face seemed lighted from within. " I cannot pass along the upper corridor without remembering afresh God's love for us all."

Unmindful of the whispering brothers below, Brother Giovanni worked on alone in silence in the upper corridor. His face shone with joy as he worked, and his brush moved, swift and sure. Suddenly his work was interrupted. A dark-robed figure approached along the corridor and paused at the painter's side. It was the abbot of the monastery, and Fra Giovanni laid down his brush, ready to listen respectfully to his superior.

"Fra Giovanni, you paint so swiftly, so beautifully," began the good abbot, who had a reason for his questions. "How can you be sure that you paint accurately?"

"Do my pictures say to you and my brothers that Jesus loved the world enough to live and die for them?" asked the little painter earnestly. "That is what my pictures must say surely and accurately."

"Yes, yes," answered the abbot with pretended impatience, "but see here" — he pointed to the picture in the first panel where Mary sat before the angel messenger listening to the promise that a Son would be born to her — "Mary never lived in such a house as this. Look, these are the round arches of this very monastery. This tiny room with its grated window might be your own cell. This little grass plot is the same one we have within our own cloistered walls. The very chair she sits on is the stool that you yourself have used."

"When I wanted to create a home for Mary, I gave to her the only home I know," explained the painter humbly, "my own monastery home. As I live here among the brothers I seem to see everything as Mary and Jesus would see it. The little flowers that spring up between the stones are beautiful with a beauty the mother of our Lord would have seen and loved. I do not know what Mary's home was like; I only know that day by day I feel as though she and the Son of God dwelt here with us."

The abbot moved past the finished pictures to the one where Fra Giovanni sat waiting to go on with his work.

"This is the picture of the great transfiguration of our Lord," he said. "But what are you doing? This little mound is not the great mountain where the Church declares the Master stood before God that day."

"I do not know what the mountain looked like on that day when the Master was transfigured," the painter spoke in low tones.

"I do not care what it looked like. I only know that my Lord was glorified that day, that he faced even the cross without fear because he loved us. See how his outflung arms remind us of his cross. In his own loved country my Lord had not where to lay his head; before him that day lay only pain and death. Perhaps he knew again the old temptation of the wilderness, and put from him, for my sake, the temptation to run from duty and so save himself. This is a picture of the Master's love for the world. Is it not a true one?" he concluded anxiously.

"And who are these two figures at the right and left?" the abbot pointed to two dimly outlined figures just under the painted faces of the great Moses and Elijah. "Surely only the two prophets were there with him, together with the three disciples."

"I think," explained the painter simply, "that our Lord's mother was never far away from him in thought. I like to picture her as always near, always sharing in his sorrow and his joy. So I painted her there near the Saviour." The painter paused a moment and then continued. "This other at the right is Saint Dominic, the Lord's servant who founded the order of which our monastery is a part. Did not all Christian grace and good begin in the presence of our Lord? My picture is not for the purpose of showing exactly how the mountain looked, nor how the people dressed, nor even to show who was there on the mountain that day. It is painted to the glory of God to show how Jesus' love for men has changed and can change a wicked world."

The good abbot touched his humble brother gently on the shoulder. "You are God's man," he whispered. "The world may never see what you have done, but we, your brothers, shall see it now and in the generations to come. Your pictures should draw us close to the Master, and we shall love and serve him the better for what you have done. Go on with your work, Brother Giovanni. The Lord himself guides your brush, as he guides your thoughts and your love."

So the painter took again the brush that he had laid aside. For six long years he painted daily in the upper corridor the pictures that reminded his brothers that the Lord was truly in their midst. When, one day, the pope sent for him to come and be a great and important archbishop, Fra Giovanni begged to be excused.

"There are many who will glory in that honor," he made answer, "but as for me, I have another work to do for my Lord."

So he worked on, painting his message of Christ's love for his comrades and for the world. When at last Giovanni's work was done and he left the monastery forever, his brothers remembered him with love, and gazed on his pictures with prayer in their hearts. As the years passed and the old brothers died and new ones came to take their places, the monks forgot the artist's name; they spoke of him as "The Blessed," or as "Brother Angel," and through his message in the pictures he lived on among them. For four hundred years the rest of the world knew nothing of these beautiful pictures of Fra Angelico, or Brother Angel, as his brothers had called him. Then one day the ancient order of monks left forever the old monastery of San Marco, and those who came after them found the pictures and shared them with the whole world. The simple message of Christ's love for all men is as real and as beautiful today as it was in the day that the pictures were painted. Italy has placed the pictures of Fra Angelico among the chiefest of its treasures and there men love to go and study them today.

A MAN WHO WORKED FOR PEACE

The man who walked through the Danish countryside was very tired. His steps lagged and his face was white with the pallor that comes from being shut away from the sun for long months at a time. This was Peter Manniche and until a few days before he had been a prisoner of the state, a prisoner because he had refused to become a soldier.

Peter Manniche was looking for something. Now and then he stopped to lean over some fence, calling greetings to the farmer or his workers.

"Good day to you, my friend," he would call. "Can you tell me where to look for a farm that I can buy? One that does not cost too much?"

Most of the time he was laughed at scornfully or good-naturedly by those who answered his greeting. These farms, with the green fields all neatly fenced in, with their stout newly painted barns, were not for sale — at least not for any price that this wanderer could pay.

At last, near Helsingör, an overalled man looked up from the row of red cabbages that he was cutting.

"A farm? Sure! Go through the town and beyond and you will find a farm to your purse's liking. Ask for Hansen's farm. It has been for sale for many a long year."

There was a chorus of laughter from the other workers. Hansen's farm! This dusty stranger could not appreciate the joke — not until he had seen the farm with his own eyes. But of course he did not know that.

"Thank you, my friend," he called gaily. "I have looked at many farms, but I have only a little money and few will sell to a man whose money is low, however high his heart."

With a new hope, Peter Manniche left the workers, who were still grinning slyly, and set out through the town to the far fields beyond. He stopped several people to ask, "Do you know where Hansen's farm lies?" but no one seemed to know.

At last Peter Manniche saw a house that looked strangely out of place among the surrounding Danish homes, though there were none so very close. This building back from the road was falling into ruins. The roof had fallen in, and if it had ever been painted at all, it was long ago. Peter's trained eye could tell that once this house had stood in the midst of broad fields, but now the stone fences had fallen and the woods beyond had crept up over the fields to the very back door. Even the little garden was lost, suffocated in the rank grass and brush.

But there was a gleam in Peter's eye as he explored the place. A little stream sang through the wood, and fell with a splash into a little pool not far from the house. He dug up some of the black earth with his fingers. It was good earth. Peter forgot how tired he was. From house to house he went throughout the neighborhood until he found the owner. Old Hansen had long been dead, he learned, and young Hansen, his son, was now a bent old man filling his pipe beside the hearth.

"For sale?" exclaimed the old man in answer to Peter's eager question. "It's been for sale so long that I forget that I own the place until the tax bill comes. Yes, you can have it, if you want it." He named a price so low that Peter's heart pounded hopefully.

"Of course, I don't have even that much money now, Mr. Hansen," he said, "but if you'll take what I have and let me pay you as I can, I want the place very much."

After the money had changed hands and the papers had been made out, Mr. Hansen plucked Peter's sleeve. "Now that the papers are passed," he said with a shrewd twinkle, "tell me, what do you want with the old place? Got any money left for tools and taxes? What can you do alone in that tangle?"

Peter grinned and then sobered suddenly. "I want to make a school there where men can learn to live with their brothers no matter what language they speak or what they call themselves. Denmark — maybe the world — needs just such a place. Once men have learned, there'll be plenty of money for plows and harrows because there won't be money needed for guns and warplanes."

The old man looked piercingly at his companion. "So!" he exclaimed. "You're Manniche, the pacifist, aren't you? Knew I'd heard your name somewhere. You've been in prison, haven't you? Should think you'd be cured of your funny ideas. Maybe I should have asked more about you before the papers passed," he grumbled. "Don't know that I like the idea of my place falling into pacifist hands. Pacifists aren't so good for Denmark," he added.

"I think what Denmark needs is a really good peacemaker," contradicted Peter with a boyish grin that showed his white teeth. "You see, Mr. Hansen," he added with a quick soberness, "I had plenty of time in prison to think about that. God made all men brothers and called them his children. Why shouldn't we live as brothers among the nations if we learn to understand one another and to work together for peace and the improvement of life wherever we find it?"

"That doesn't sound like pacifist talk," said young Hansen scratching his gray head. "Sounds like good sense, and who ever heard of a pacifist with good sense? You went to prison because you were a traitor. Forgot that?"

"Men called me so," said Peter sadly, "but I love my king and my country. I love all men too well to want to maim or kill them.

I want to help them. No man has a right to call himself a peacemaker unless he wants to do something to help men to live together in peace. Your farm is going to give me a chance to show you what a peacemaker can really do."

In spite of the old man's doubts, Peter could hardly wait to begin work. He shared his plans with one or two close friends and they helped. The old house was made watertight, given a coat of paint, and cleaned up. Brush was cut down around the house and the little pool was cleaned out. The garden was coaxed into bloom, and one field was cleared, plowed, and sown with good wheat. There were money problems, but there was something about Peter Manniche that made people trust him. With his first harvest he paid his bills and had enough left to buy a cow. He and a growing group of enthusiastic friends cut down logs and trimmed them and built a barn for the cow.

A great deal of work went into that farm and much prayer, and today, just outside Helsingör, stands the International People's College, a place where men and women from all over the world came to make friends and to work and live together before the Second World War. More and more land was cleared, for part of the way in which one paid expenses at this school was to work to make the school a finer place. Men who did not understand each other's language shared a room together and worked side by side in the fields or building a new barn. They listened to talks in various languages by stouthearted Christian leaders. They spent time learning languages and teaching one another under the trees, or as they sat together at the table. They worshiped together in the chapel, glad that they had one Father, God, who draws all men to him and to one another.

One summer Peter Manniche invited a learned English college professor to come and teach and help in his school. The professor arrived at People's College with all his bags and a large trunk. To his surprise no one was at the depot to meet him, though he had sent word when he should arrive. To make matters more irritating, he found the school office empty, and polite inquiries as to the whereabouts of Peter Manniche brought forth only, "He must be outside somewhere." With some distaste he wandered out of doors and over the fields. The green grass was dotted with daisies, and the barns looked clean and trim in their new coats of red paint. A mother duck quacked encouragingly to a little brood that dotted the pond with yellow. In a bean field a group of men were hard at work.

"Can you tell me where I can find Peter Manniche, the headmaster?" he inquired.

A tall man in overalls straightened up and stepped over the rows of beans with great bare feet. His blond, straight hair was standing on end in the breeze.

"I am Peter Manniche," he grinned. "And you?"

"Well!" the professor could not hide his surprise. "I am the English master you asked to come over and help you this summer." Even Peter's friendly smile and warm handclasp could not dispel the learned man's distaste. Imagine! A headmaster in bare feet and overalls working like any laborer in the fields!

Peter Manniche seized his visitor's arm and took him to the barn and showed him the rows of fat, scrubbed cows and the half dozen new calves, but the Englishman was scarcely interested. The men milking the cows, Peter said, were some German students, one of them from the old Heidelberg University.

"College students milking cows!" echoed the learned professor. "I say, old fellow, this is all very nice, but really you know —"

Peter Manniche was not listening. "I am so glad you have come," he said. "We need you so. We have a number of English students and several Jewish schoolteachers from New York here, and my English — well, she is not so good." His eyes crinkled in a smile.

"But surely you do not expect me to work in the fields and milk cows!" cried the professor, thinking of his trunk filled with riding clothes. There was a Tuxedo and a white linen suit for boating there also. In fact, he was sure that he had nothing at all suitable to wear for his new work, if this was a fair sample.

"We want you to do whatever you think will help us most," said Peter simply, and the warm pressure of his fingers on his visitor's arm was as friendly as ever. "We need so much help, and so many kinds of help. Please make your own plan and do whatever you think is most needed."

Back in his room (the professor found that he was rooming with a Bulgarian whose only understandable language was a hearty handshake and a look of welcome in his dark eyes), he had to make up his mind what to do. Should he go home without unpacking? He could just imagine the dress suit and yachting whites hung next to the rough woolen best coat and the clean spare overalls of his roommate!

Somehow the learned Englishman found that Peter was hard to forget. His friendly touch was still warm on his arm. He stayed. Peter lent him some overalls and a warm sweater, and soon he was helping to prune the apple orchard in the mornings and lecturing in the afternoons. Before the summer was over he had helped his comrades as they worked out together a plan for a silo. Proudly he took a real part in the building of it.

That was seven years before the Second World War, but every summer after that he spent with Peter Manniche and his international students. Into every country of Europe, and even into North and South America, these men carried a new idea of world brotherhood and what it means to live in the world as children of a common Father.

In the midst of wars and hate it is certain that Peter Manniche is still at work somewhere. Perhaps there are fewer men who listen to him; perhaps his school is facing a testing time such as we cannot know. Of one thing we can be sure. Because Peter Manniche's faith is great, his work cannot fail. It may be that his work will help toward making a lasting peace and Christ-like living possible for all men. For Peter Manniche is a stalwart follower of the Lord Jesus, and has unlimited faith in the power of his Leader.

JEW AND GENTILE [1]

One day I turned up a street to make a call. Three houses from the corner there was a garden gate on which a Nazi slogan about the vileness of Jews had been painted. It was Easter morning. The paint was yellow. A boy of perhaps fourteen was scrubbing it off. He was a tall, straight, blond, blue-eyed boy. He had a square head. His eyes were hard, in the way that a Prussian's eyes can be hard.

[1] From "Marching Through the Mulberries," by Nora Waln. *The Saturday Evening Post,* July 1, 1939. Used by permission.

He was a stranger to me. I asked him a question, because this is my habit wherever I encounter that which arouses my curiosity. My question was, "Have you Jewish blood?"

His gaze pierced me like a sword. "Should it concern you, my inheritance is what the Nazis are pleased to call 'pure Aryan.'"

He continued to scrub, using a stiff brush and turpentine. I persisted, "Then why do you clean this off?"

He swung around, clicking his heels together. "Because this is a crime against my fatherland."

Our scene had attracted the attention of a man in brown uniform who came out of a house across the street. He walked up to us and asked, "What's going on here?"

The boy acted unconscious of his presence.

The man gave a command: "Cease to remove that paint. Get a can of fresh paint from my house. Rewrite what you have destroyed."

The boy finished the word he was erasing. He straightened from his task and turned slowly until his eyes caught the gaze of the man who had addressed him. It was the man who moved uneasily, dropping his eyes. Only when he had made the man do it did the boy speak.

He said, "I come of German patriots who do not have their duty told to them."

To my surprise, the man in brown uniform went back to his house. I made my call at the end of the street. When I came back, there was no yellow paint on that garden gate. No one stood there.

This occurred two years ago. When I last heard of this boy, he was still following that same direct course. He had not faltered, although there lie across his path the dangers of arrest at any moment, imprisonment without trial indefinitely, the tortures of concentration camp, or, as has happened to other youth like him, death on the executioner's block with his name publicly branded by the Nazi Government as that of a traitor and no explanation of his crime.

FOLLOWERS OF GOOD WILL

The hot June sun poured down on the crowds of homeless and hopeless refugees that pressed about the Friends' Canteen somewhere in France. Now and then a kind of dreadful stillness fell on them as the air around them shook with the vibrations of heavy guns. The kindly French people found little time to think of what the sound might mean for them as they watched with great pity the hordes of refugees pouring into their city — Austrian, Jew, Dutch, American, German, Belgian, and a dozen other nationalities — whom war had torn from their homes. No one stopped these hopeless folk, but the kindly French did what they could to welcome them all. Even that hard day when news came of the surrender of King Leopold of Belgium, which trapped their French and English comrades, the French people by neither word nor action showed ill will. They treated the Belgian refugees as they treated their own.

Under the direction of the little group of Quakers in charge of the Canteen, friend and enemy shared alike, and the French who remained in the city brought every potato and grain of wheat that they could possibly spare and added them to the meager store of supplies which must feed these hungry strangers. They were too busy helping to think of the roads black with refugees pouring in and out of the city by every exit. Among them were members of some of their own families, who fled before the roar of guns which was growing louder every day. If all of them ran away what would happen to these old men and crying babies, to the weary mothers and bewildered, half-grown boys and girls who had fled for days through the sunbaked countryside before the sound of guns? In all the city there was scarcely one who remained in his place who did not know in his heart that it was only a matter of days, perhaps of hours, before the gray hordes of the enemy would pour into the city. These were too numerous and too strong for the weary defenders to cope with. The tension was spreading, and even the Canteen workers, trying so desperately to help, did not escape it altogether. At last the worker in charge called her helpers together.

"We must decide," she said quietly, "what we want to do. It

is dangerous here. The German advance is steady and unbroken; soon they will be in the city. If we go immediately, we may make our way to safety and comfort; but there will be no coming back, and these helpless people must face whatever comes with no one to care for them. If we stay, we must face danger with them, but it is the only way that we can maintain contact with them or hope to win official German consent to continue our work. We must decide now what we will do."

The little group of Friends were silent, and in his own way each opened his mind and heart to the leading of the Master in whose service they were; each was ready to go or to stay as seemed best. This war was not of their making; Friends make war only on war itself. But though they did not take sides with French or German, though they spoke of battles and persecution only to warn against them, they offered their help wherever it was needed and called no man enemy. The German refugee was cared for in his turn as quickly as the native Frenchman, his wounds as carefully dressed, his family as wisely counseled. If they, the Friends, fled to safety, who would stand to help impartially here where all needed help? Anxiously the refugees and their few remaining French helpers waited. At last in the still room one spoke.

"There are those here whose responsibilities force them to seek safety for the sake of those who depend on them, but as for me, I shall stay."

"And I!"

"And I!"

"Count on me also."

"And on me!"

And so it was that the little group of Christians who called themselves Friends stayed on while the guns roared more and more loudly and thick palls of dust and smoke rolled over the city. Steadily the Friends stayed at their post while lumbering tanks tore their way through the last barrier, while the last of the defenders threw down their arms in defeat, while gray lines of marching men tramped into the city as conquerors. Fear gripped the refugees, and many hid themselves or ran on again leaving the conquered city behind them, but the Friends spoke reassuringly to those who stayed, set them to work caring for the sick and for the children who could not care for themselves. Belgian and Austrian sat down together to peel the great sacks of potatoes and drop them in the thickening stew that was stirred by other hands. Little by little it was fear that fled, and little by little a new confidence grew where there had been none. The gray hordes marching past were only men after all, like themselves. They too were weary and hungry and perhaps not unacquainted with fear. A nurse bound up a bleeding German arm; no one growled that this was helping the enemy; it was just a great something that was reaching out and out, farther and farther, until it brought a new hope to all that it touched.

"These Friends," whispered a Jew to the Austrian who worked beside him, "they are like the love of God that is for all men!"

The other nodded. "They keep hope alive in a crazy world," he answered. "To them all men are alike and all alike must be served."

"It was so the Nazarene taught," replied the other slowly. "They are a little like him, I think."

It was not always easy to keep alive and working the spirit of impartial concern for all. The Quaker workers had their opinion of the cruelties and injustices that war always brings. Some felt their sympathies going out to the conquered and knew the need to struggle against feelings of resentment and anger toward the conquerors. But, whatever their thoughts, they gave their help where help was most needed. "We are not helping this nation or that," they explained quietly when questions were asked. "We are helping *people*." These Friends had nothing to sell, nothing to gain for themselves; they had only a great outpouring of good will to share with all.

Gifts of money and clothing came from Christians of many faiths all over America. Even so, there came a time when food and money began to give out and when it was apparent that there could not be enough for all. Then it was the weaker and more needy ones to whom the Friends turned.

"If we cannot do all that we would, then we must do what we can," they said. So, where many workers would have given up in despair because the need was so great and the helpers and resources were so few, this little company of Christians worked steadily on. If there was an ache in their hearts they hid it as best they could. "There are a hundred hungry children for whom we have no food," they said gravely. "But we have enough to share with this child, and with this one and this one," picking out the very ones who needed help most.

When it was time to try to settle their refugees into crowded quarters, there was trouble at first. Some French families felt that they could not live with the Belgians who had surrendered, and so, they said, betrayed them into the enemy's hands. The Dutch and the Spanish could remember a long-ago war between their two lands which still rankled, and they did not think that they should be asked to share the same tents. Some Austrians and some Jews who remembered long-ago unkindness and injustice felt that they could not stay together. "Why should not the people of each nationality have their own tents, and their own dishes and their own food?" they asked.

The Quaker workers gathered the people together in smaller groups. They were so friendly themselves, so appreciative of the worth-while and the noble that is to be found in every nation, that before long the Dutch were singing Spanish songs and Austrian artists were painting pictures of Jewish people playing and working in their old homes. Ancient enmities were being forgotten and new friendships were being made.

"It is the Christian way of things," one would explain to a surprised newcomer. "It is the right way."

At home in America there were some who wondered about this. They could see no point to be gained by being friendly to those who are not friendly themselves.

"We will help to feed these refugees, or those," they said, "but why should we bother to help those who have been so cruel and unjust? Why be concerned when misfortune falls upon those who abuse another people because they are little or because they are in the way of the conquerors?"

But the Friends had an answer for that. "We cannot pick our particular places and peoples to whom good will will be sent," they explained. "Good will that is like in kind to the good will our Leader had for the world must go everywhere, wherever there is need; it must call no man enemy."

One day the worker in charge of the local unit working for the refugees had an emergency call from another worker to the south in unoccupied France. She must go, but how should it be arranged? If she left that part of France where the Germans were in full charge, perhaps they would not let her in again. Perhaps they would not let her go to her fellow workers' aid in any case. Well, one can always try. She went to the headquarters of the new German commandant in charge of that part of occupied France. There at the door was a long line of people waiting to see the military governor. "No," she was told, she could not hope to see the commandant before four o'clock of that afternoon; it was then early in the morning and time was very precious.

Quietly she slipped around to a side door. A sentry stopped her.

"Halt!" he demanded sternly. "Do you not know that it is forbidden to enter here?"

"I am the Friend in charge of the work being done here for the refugees. I must go to southern France immediately to help another Friend who is working there. I want the commandant's permission."

The sentry saluted, and stepped aside.

"Go to the third door on the right," he said. "Tell the officer in charge who you are, and he will help you."

The worker hurried to obey and, to her delight, the officer in charge, on hearing who she was, went himself to the commandant and returned speedily. He brought with him full permission to go where she would, at any time she wished, and to take with her any companion helper she wanted. She could not understand such generosity.

"It is simple," smiled the officer. "You see, when I was a child, and my wife was a child, we were fed by the Quakers after the terrible days of the last war. We know that your work is one of honest good will, and that you serve as a friend, not of the French, nor of the Germans, but as a friend of all mankind. Such good will cannot be hindered or delayed. The commandant understands; these papers will open any road for you." And, saluting her smartly, the officer turned back to his work.

So the work went on. Babies were fed with needed milk; sick children were given cocoa and rice to add to their meager food rations. There were beds set up for the sick and shelter was found for the homeless. Of course the best that the Friends could do still left hundreds and hundreds of refugees for whom nothing could be done, but no one thought of giving up.

"If we cannot do all that we should like to," the Friends told one another, "that is no excuse for not doing everything that we can. Perhaps — who knows — if we can just keep going what we have started, more help may come from America and these others will find hope too."

Perhaps — perhaps they were remembering another Friend long ago who was pressed about by crowds that were too great for him to heal and help as much as he would have liked to; nevertheless, he did what he could without thought of his own comfort or safety. It is what he expects of all who would themselves be friends of his.

FRIENDS AT NEIGHBORHOOD HOUSE [1]

"You're it! You're it!" yelled Tony as he caught Maria, the new girl, and tagged her.

The other players ran in all directions, expecting another merry chase, but the new girl just stood there in the center of the floor all by herself. She looked frightened. Suddenly she burst into tears!

The boys and girls gazed at her in surprise. Why should anyone cry because she was tagged? Didn't she know that it was part of the game? They did not know what to do, so they just stood and stared.

Just then Miss Johnson, the teacher in charge at Neighborhood House, came in. Tony hurried to her, followed by Rachel and Karl and Olga and Henry.

"Maria won't play — she just cried," explained Tony.

"Tony wasn't rough, Miss Johnson," added Olga. "He was playing fair."

"She's new, and we thought she would *want* to be it. I would," Henry said.

"Yes, I am sure you wanted to make her feel at home," Miss Johnson answered. "But the first thing to do now is to try to find out what is the matter."

[1] By Mary Alice Jones.

Miss Johnson went over to the frightened little girl, standing alone in the middle of the floor. She took her by the hand. Why, the child was trembling! Maria wasn't ready to play.

"Would you like to come with me for a little while, dear, and see some new kittens we have in the basement?"

Maria looked up, but she did not smile. Miss Johnson looked at the other children and motioned to them to go on with their game, as she led the little girl away.

After a while she came back alone, and the boys and girls ran up to ask her about some new games. They had forgotten the little girl who cried. But Miss Johnson hadn't. She explained that Maria was taking a nap.

"How would you like a story instead of another game?" she asked, and the children sat on the floor, eager for a new story.

"Not so very long ago," began Miss Johnson, "there was a little girl who lived in an attic. It wasn't a nice play attic, but a very hot attic. The little girl had to stay there all day. She had never in all her life seen a flower growing, for the attic was in a large city. Her mother was so busy all day making paper flowers that she had no time to take her little girl out to see the real flowers. The little girl had to help to make the paper flowers too. Her mother would go early in the morning to the factory and get the bright-colored leaves and petals and wire. Then all day, and often during the evening, the mother and the little girl wrapped wire and bound petals and leaves together to make artificial flower bouquets. At first, the little girl thought that the gay colors were pretty and she liked making the big bouquets. But after doing it all day long for many days, her fingers grew sore and her eyes ached and her back was tired and her legs were cramped from sitting still so long.

"Sometimes the wire slipped and cut her fingers, but there was no time to stop and bind them up; so they became very sore. The mother was sorry that her little girl didn't have time to play, but the factory paid so little for the flowers that it took all that she and the little girl could make by working all day to pay the rent for the attic and buy food.

"And then one day a caller came to the attic. The lady looked at the little girl. She knew that children should play and be in the sunshine and have milk to drink. And so the lady began to

THE STORY SECTION

make plans. She talked with some friends at her church, and they decided that the church should help. They found a new job for the mother in the next town. They brought the little girl to the home of a friend of ours, who lives next door, to stay during the week while her mother is at work."

The story was finished and the children looked at Miss Johnson. "They brought the little girl to Mrs. Craig's house?" they asked. They all liked Mrs. Craig. Miss Johnson nodded.

"I know," exclaimed Tony after a second. "I know — the little girl is Maria." The other children looked at Miss Johnson and she said, "Yes."

"You see, Mrs. Craig thought it would be fine for Maria to come to Neighborhood House to play because she had never had a place to play before."

"But we were noisy and scared her," broke in Olga.

"I'll bet she didn't even know what it meant when Tony tagged her," added Henry.

"And she was too tired to run anyway, if she hadn't had any milk and things," Karl went on.

"All that you have said is true," Miss Johnson admitted. "Maria was frightened, and she didn't know how to play tag. She is weak too. Of course, Mrs. Craig gave her a nice lunch when she came today, but one lunch couldn't make up for so many, many days when she didn't have the right food."

"Well, what shall we do?" asked Tony. "Can we go over and teach her to play?"

"No," announced Rachel. "What we ought to do is to help her to get strong first. Then we can teach her games. I think we should make her a health book, showing her what she ought to eat to get strong — with pictures, you know, Miss Johnson."

"Like the ones we made for ourselves to help us to be strong when we first came to Neighborhood House," added Olga.

"Why, that would be a fine plan," agreed Miss Johnson.

"We can make one right away, and take it over and leave it with Mrs. Craig to give to her," Henry proposed.

"Then she will know that we want to be friends," Tony said.

And so the boys and girls went to work right away. They found in old magazines some lovely pictures of vegetables and oatmeal and macaroni and milk and orange juice and soup and all other good things to eat that make boys and girls strong and healthy. They found their paste and scissors and soon were mounting the pictures on sheets of wrapping paper that Tony had cut to the right size. Then they found a piece of cardboard for the cover and pasted on it a picture of Neighborhood House and wrote under it: "To Maria. From your friends at Neighborhood House."

When the book was delivered Maria looked at it in surprise. She had never had a picture book in all her life! Mrs. Craig explained about the food pictures and why the boys and girls had sent it, and then she and Maria planned their supper right out of the picture book.

Every afternoon during the play hour at Neighborhood House the other boys and girls asked about Maria. Was she getting better? Were her hands well again? When could she come to play with them? After a few weeks Maria did come again. The boys and girls could scarcely believe that she was the same little girl. She was fatter, and her cheeks rosier, and she didn't look the least bit afraid. Miss Johnson brought her into the room, and the other girls and boys all came up and told her their names, and she smiled and looked as if she wanted to be friends.

"I liked my book," she said shyly.

"Let's play 'hide-and-seek,'" suggested Olga.

"Oh, that's baby —" began Tony, but Rachel punched him.

"It's got to be an easy one to begin with," she explained in a whisper. Tony caught on.

"Oh, sure," he said generously. "That's a fine game."

And so Maria began to play for the first time in her life. The other boys and girls were very kind to her. They knew how it felt to be afraid. They remembered the first time that they had come to Neighborhood House. They remembered how they had had to learn to eat the right foods to get strong and healthy, for Neighborhood House had taught all the boys and girls and their mothers lots of things that they hadn't known about health, and playing fair, and sharing, and being kind.

Maria learned so fast that before long she was the very best runner on the Neighborhood House playgrounds! She won the race in the track meet. All the boys and girls were glad, because they liked her.

General Plans for Conducting the Department

ORGANIZING THE JUNIOR DEPARTMENT OF THE SCHOOL

For a Junior Department of ten to twelve Juniors one teacher and possibly one assistant will be sufficient, provided that one of these can play the piano. They would share the telling of stories, leading of discussions, and guidance of group activities. For more than twelve Juniors an additional assistant would be advisable for each eight or ten children. One of these assistants should be a person especially interested in handcrafts.

If thirty or more Juniors are in the department, room to allow for grading is practically a necessity. Activities may be graded according to their difficulty, and the Juniors divided into grades for planning and working. If a grade has more than twelve or fifteen children, the teacher will need an assistant. Mothers willing to serve can often be found, if not too much time is asked of them outside of school time. Should space and leadership or small enrollment make it unwise to divide the department into three grades, it may still be possible to have a younger and an older group of Juniors, numbering not more than twelve or fifteen in each group.

In small schools where all departments gather in one room, there may be space out of doors or in the pastor's study where groups can meet; some near-by interested church member may be persuaded to offer his porch, woodshed, or barn floor for the use of small working groups. In a certain rural Vacation School the Juniors, who found the one-room Church School crowded, divided into groups and each adopted a favorite apple tree in a near-by orchard. With the farmer's consent, each group carried out planed boards and horses and set up its own worktables every sunny day. In rainy weather the Juniors used the church pews as worktables, covering them carefully with clean newspapers, and kneeling or sitting on low stools before them. Heavy cardboard cut into pieces fifteen by eighteen inches makes admirable lapboards, or the boards can be leaned against the pew before which each Junior sits or kneels for work.

If the Junior Department of the school has its own room, tables in various corners or along well-lighted walls may be placed for special purposes: for notebook work, drawing, and painting; for reading and making notes; or for conference or exhibit purposes, according to the plans which children and leaders may make for them. If tables are limited in number, a reading corner can be arranged where there is good light and where readers will not interfere with others or be interfered with, and where chairs, or stools, and orange-crate bookcases (painted by the children) invite them to be at home. A board laid across two orange crates makes a very satisfactory table.

As often as may be necessary the principal will call her teachers and other workers into conference for planning. Suggestions for the workers' conference are given on page 167.

KEEPING DEPARTMENT RECORDS

There is value in the keeping of complete school records. The records should be simple, free of all extraneous information which is of no value to the school. Perhaps the inclusion of each child's name, address, age, nationality, and the church membership of his parents are the only facts needed by the school, and by those responsible for a later follow-up of the school's work. These records may be kept on small lined cards, 3" x 5", such as can be bought in the five-and-ten, or the records can be kept in a loose-leaf notebook. The pages can be ruled into squares for the convenient entry of attendance. On the back of the cards or in the back pages of the record book, needed facts as to special problems in connection with any of the children can be noted. Or records of observations made on some desirable evidence of growth or ability can be made. For example, the teacher may need a reminder that " Mary Smith has just moved into the neighborhood, and has never been to Sunday School before." When Mary Smith's work or background of knowledge presents mysterious lapses, the record may explain why. Or perhaps some assistant has noted that Tim O'Neil is particularly good in helping the little fellows on the playground. It may help to know this when committees are made up, or when the school director wants someone to help the Primary boys to organize a new game at recess.

A record of all expenses for supplies, equipment, outings, and other payments filed at the close of the school will prove of great help to those responsible for the reopening of the school another year.

PLANNING FOR THE CARE OF DEPARTMENT SUPPLIES

A suggested list of basic supplies is given on page 177; for the rest much will depend upon group planning as the work of the school gets under way. The Juniors will co-operate enthusiastically about such matters as bringing cracker tins for the safekeeping of crayons and mayonnaise or jelly jars for holding paint supplies. Paintbrushes can be kept in a glass jar, brush end up. If there is a Junior supply committee, the members will want to see that brushes are always carefully cleaned each time before they are put away. Muffin tins may be used for mixing paints for immediate use.

Each type of supply should be kept by itself, either on its own shelf or half shelf or in boxes which have been labeled as to contents. For example, there might be a carton marked "paints"; another marked "drawing paper"; and so forth. The Juniors may make envelopes to keep their individual or committee work in, or they may bring shopping bags from home, on which they have pasted an identifying picture or, better still, printed their names. There should be a special place or shelf space where these envelopes or bags can be kept.

PLANNING FOR THE WORKERS' CONFERENCE

There is a great deal of detailed planning to be done if the school is to run smoothly. This planning involves every worker in the school whether these be two or twenty. If possible, every worker should attend a training class for Vacation Church School teachers. The entire staff should meet at least once or twice before the opening of the school. This is to make sure that every worker knows exactly in what room or in what part of a room she will meet her group, and where supplies are. It will also mean that every worker not only knows the general program of the school but has a real part in planning it. In a preliminary conference or series of conferences such questions as the following must be considered:

Where will pupils be sent for enrollment and who will enroll them? Does the one responsible know how this is to be done?

What part of record-keeping will each department be expected to care for? (Probably the daily attendance of each child will be the main record for which the department will be held responsible.) How will the department records be collected for the school's permanent file?

What are the special problems of the first day of school? In what specific ways can each worker best help with these?

What is the major responsibility of each worker on the staff? (The staff will need to know who will be responsible for playing the piano, telling the stories, supervising the play period, working with special committees [see list of Junior committees following]. Probably some of these assignments will be permanent responsibilities and some rotated. In planning the assignments much will depend upon the interest and abilities of the various workers.)

At what hour will each department of the school have the use of the playground, the washrooms, the chapel if needed?

What equipment must be shared by two or more departments? What is the best plan for sharing this and for caring for it?

When and where is our first staff conference to be held after school has started?

Besides these preliminary conferences, involving the co-operative planning for the whole school, the Junior Department teacher will doubtless want to meet her own assistants. Responsibilities for collecting materials and for preparing to guide interest groups should be allotted among the department workers. Again personal interests and individual abilities should determine the placing of responsibility. The assistants clever in design and sewing will obviously be best able to help groups working on notebook covers or making costumes for a play. The assistant who excels

GENERAL PLANS FOR THE DEPARTMENT   169

in sports, who likes to hike and plan outdoor activities, will be immensely valuable on the playground. She should be a person who understands the opportunities play and activity offer for Christian decisions and actions on the part of the Juniors and how to utilize these wisely. That department is most fortunate whose workers have something that they are enthusiastic about which they are able to share with boys and girls. The teacher may need to add a word of warning, however, to enthusiastic assistants, lest they tend to "put over" on boys and girls their own particular interests, regardless of possible boy and girl interests. It is important also that every assistant see the work of the school as a whole, and feel herself or himself responsible for the total program. Nothing is more disrupting to the unified work of the school than for assistants who carry special responsibilities to come into the school and carry out their particular "act" without reference to what has been going on in the rest of the day's work.

IS A TIME SCHEDULE NEEDED?

Every member of the staff will doubtless have a tentative schedule in mind as she plans her day's work, but it must be kept in mind that no one can be sure ahead of time as to the exact amount of time needed for various activities. The department teacher is responsible for seeing that the day's session is well balanced, so that there is both variety and stability. This means seeing that everyone is interested and working at something worth while; it means that the Juniors have time for planning, for consultation and experimenting, and for bringing work to a reasonable completeness before having to leave it for something else. The more flexible the time schedule in a department, the more care is needed in planning.

The usual session length in a Vacation School is from two and a half to three hours. For convenience in planning, a possible morning program is given below, not with the thought that any school will adopt and adhere to it, but merely as a suggestion of what a well-planned session ought to include in proportion to the time available. It assumes that school opens at 9.00 A.M. and closes at 12.00. In some localities schools begin at 8.30 and close at 11.30, because of the excessive midday heat. Where desired, a five-minute warning should be given before the end of the work period so that the Juniors will be able to plan good stopping places.

8.30 to 9.00. Arrival of the workers, who begin the day with prayer, followed by the assembling of materials and getting ready for the morning's work. The play supervisor will of course go immediately to the playground to welcome the arriving children. Many of the best learning experiences of the day will come as the children begin their living together in play; the supervisor must be ready at all times to utilize the values of these play experiences. Special suggestions are provided for the play supervisor on page 30.

9.00 to 9.30. Opening of the school with informal planning and working period. Committees carrying responsibilities should care for them during this time. The room committee may arrange the room according to the requirements of work under way. There may be a schedule on the blackboard, so that the Juniors can readily check up on the progress of their work, evaluate completed parts of the work, and make new assignments. Also, they will want to make a record of new work agreed upon, or changes to be made in work that has been judged and found wanting. There should be ample time for continuing work on enterprises already under way.

9.30 to 10.45. This period will probably be divided into two parts, except where trips or outside investigations are to be made; for these the whole period may be necessary. Ordinarily, a part of this period will be given over to stories, discussions, supervised study involving the use of the materials in the Juniors' reading corner, planning for or reporting on excursions, investigations to be made or having been made, memorization of Biblical passages, picture studies, and sharing experiences, during which reports of findings will be shared and discussed and perhaps plans for using some of them will be made. A second part of this period will be needed for creative work, such as writing, making miniature scenes, working on dramatizations, making scenery and costumes, and carrying out other related enterprises. Provision should be made in this period for free choices so that each pupil will have an opportunity to follow out some chosen interest which

GENERAL PLANS FOR THE DEPARTMENT

will contribute to rather than interfere with what others are doing. It is for this reason that so full and varied a list of pupil activities has been included on pages 185–197.

The period will not necessarily be divided in the above order, for the creative period might well come first, but provision for both types of work should be found in this class period.

10.45 to 11.00. Clean-up period, and rearrangement of room for the next part of the program.

11.00 to 11.30. Supervised play — out of doors if weather permits.

11.30 to 11.40. Preparation for worship. This short period should prove one of the most valuable parts of the morning session, where there can be developed a knowledge of and love for some of our choicest hymns, poetry, litanies, and similar religious material commonly used in worship. Here will be made occasional explanations of the real meaning and purposes of worship; here, from time to time, without preachiness or tacked-on moralizations, peak points in the daily program growing out of problems and out of new and happy experiences will be utilized in motivating worship. This is the time to discuss the purpose of the offering, if one is regularly taken, and good ways of making the offering a genuine part of worship. Perhaps in this period the members of the group will want to prepare together a litany or prayer to be used in their own worship.

11.40 to 12.00. Quiet music, meditation, and worship. (Some schools may prefer to begin their school with worship. There is no " best time " for this; each school may plan its own worship time.)

USING JUNIOR COMMITTEES

The success of a Vacation School is largely determined not by pupil interest but also by the responsibility pupils tak seeing that it runs smoothly and well. In their own depar Juniors can do much to keep the work moving forward care they take of working materials, by the making of reg concerning the use of these and other equipment, by themselves responsible for such things as the care of the planning of some of the games, and the planning and ing of some of the worship services.

Committees should be changed frequently, so that all have an opportunity to serve on them and also because interest is kept alive by variety of work. A week is a good length of time for each committee to serve. All committees should be encouraged to work out their own plans for caring for their responsibilities without waiting for prompting. They need to know, however, that they are always free to consult with teacher or assistant when faced with a problem that calls for advice. As work gets under way and groups begin to plan special projects or activities, these groups may want to call themselves " committees " whose responsibilities will continue until the specific project is completed, but such " committee " work must be left to pupil planning. The suggestions for continued committee responsibility which follow are indicative of what might be of real value both to the department work and to the development of pupil initiative and responsibility.

The Game Committee. Such a committee might be responsible for planning one or more games for each day for a week. (For game suggestions see page 178.) Plans should include readiness to show patience in making explanations, effort to see that all have an equal chance to play and that no one child or group gets all the opportunities to play " leader " or some other desirable part in a game. Such a committee will want to see that younger or new children are helped to become a part of the playing group and, in co-operation with the play supervisor, will want to work out some definite play purposes for presentation to the group as a whole. This committee might assume a major responsibility in seeing that there is open discussion of any reasons why play does not go smoothly and how Juniors can improve conditions. The play supervisor will work closely with this committee and will help the members to see that the way play is carried on is important to Juniors who are trying to discover what living as followers of Jesus means.

The Worship Committee. These Juniors will need to see that the place where worship is to take place is made just as attractive as possible each day. If they do not have the use of an extra room, there is still much that can be done to make the department room pleasant and cheerful. Summer gardens can supply flowers, or wild flowers are abundant in the country.

Sometimes a worship center can be planned, with a picture to help to create the right atmosphere. Always the room should be clean. As there comes to be a body of content through which the Juniors have previously worshiped and as daily preparation for worship adds meaning to the experience, this committee may on occasion help to plan and to conduct some of the services of worship, or to assist the leader of worship through readiness to be called upon for telling stories, for reading from the Bible, and for any other suitable share in helping to add to the spirit and enjoyment of worship.

The Room Committee. This committee will want each day to get the room ready for work and to see that it is left in good order at the close of each session. Tables where painting or pasting is done may need to be covered for protection of their surface. Wastebaskets should be kept emptied, plants and flowers watered. Perhaps there is a window garden to be cared for; or a place for the safekeeping of the lizard, turtle, or tadpole which Juniors often bring to such a school may need to be provided. Such creatures must be cared for intelligently, and their proper feeding and care might be a part of the duty of a room committee.

The Supply Committee. Members of this committee will need to be on hand early to see that all needed supplies are in readiness for use, and conveniently placed. They should keep track of supplies to see that the teacher is informed if paint, paper, or other material is running low. Check needs to be made each day to see that paintbrushes are clean, books returned to their proper places, and the supply closet or shelf in good order. The committee may feel the need of drawing up some rules about the care and use of supplies. Such rules should be posted in the closet or on the door. Books should be mended when necessary.

PREPARING TO TEACH THIS COURSE

A teacher's attitude toward her work will determine largely its success or failure. If she thinks of the room or corner where she meets her group as the place where she will tell the children "things for their own good" or "things that they ought to know," if she thinks of "a good Junior" only as one who listens passively, gives the expected answers, and does as he is told, then her school will do little to enrich the lives of her Juniors. Being told what is right and good, with no chance in the school to put it to use, is not the way to develop strong, responsible Christian character. Good Juniors are Juniors who are actively at work, thinking, planning, doing, discussing, studying, because of their own sense of need to know; good Juniors are Juniors who take responsibility for what they think and say and do, and face that responsibility constructively; good Juniors are much concerned with judging what they have done and in planning next steps. This is what makes for true learning and growing; there are no short cuts. One can recite accurately the whole of the Sermon on the Mount, but if its principles do not take hold of the reciter in such a way as to change his way of thinking and acting, he has not truly learned them. Real learning takes place only when what we have learned changes us in some way.

So, as the teacher gets ready to teach, she thinks first of her Juniors as *people*, persons who have experiences, who think and choose and act and react in relation to all that goes on about them. She will plan to find out all she can about her Juniors. She will visit their homes, talk to their parents and Church School teachers, and perhaps to public-school teachers and social workers who know these boys and girls. Most of all, she will keep alert to know them by the best means of all, living with them as a member of their group as they work and discuss and make plans together.

The wise teacher will not be afraid that she may not know all there is to know about this matter of following Christ; she will not even be afraid to say to her questioning pupils, "I don't know the answer to these questions, but perhaps we can find out some of these things together this summer, for I want to study and work with you too." The best of all teachers is the one who is herself a growing Christian personality; she does not have to know all the answers but she does need an open mind and a desire to learn and to prepare herself to guide boys and girls in growing as Christians.

A good teacher will not do anything for her Juniors that they are able to do for themselves. She will think of herself as more experienced, and so as a valuable contributor to the group, but she will refrain from making all the decisions, choosing all the games, choosing all the activities, or doing the summing up after discussion. She must have a goal, and know clearly just what it is that she is trying to accomplish; all the questions that she asks, all the stories that she tells, all the opportunities for thinking and planning that she can provide for her group must contribute to her goal. Yet she will welcome the way the Juniors word their own goals, though they will differ from her way. She will be eager to accept suggestions from the pupils, even if it means changing her plans at certain points. She will call attention to good work wherever she finds it, not by praising it superficially, but by helping the pupils to make good use of it and by showing her own appreciation of it. She will hold high standards for herself, and so guide her group that they will never be satisfied with second-best thinking and workmanship; she will use great care in seeing that the Juniors do not set a standard so high as to be utterly beyond their ability to attain in some measure. Above all, she will avoid arousing in her pupils any great emotional reaction which cannot find avenues for outpouring in worship, in service, in right attitudes and actions toward others in the group, or in some other way. Nothing is deadlier to the development of wholesome Christian character than to arouse emotion without providing some means of using that emotion constructively.

A good teacher depends on group discussion and thinking, rather than upon moralizing, to insure pupil learning; that is, she will not lecture about bad habits and conduct when she has led her group to think about and to discuss Christian principles of living. To do that is to take advantage, to make the Juniors feel that they have been caught unfairly, and it will tend to make them very wary about committing themselves in the future when the leader tries to get them to discuss such matters. The best discussion leader is one who refrains from expressing approval or disapproval of Junior statements, for they have not yet had sufficient experience to have many convictions or to maintain these regardless of the opinions of others; they tend, therefore, to say what they think will win the approval and praise of the leader instead of thinking for themselves. A good discussion leader will not push Juniors in an effort to make them come to conclusions before they are ready for it; rather, she will encourage boys and girls to return again to a discussion of an idea and to think about and discuss it outside of school. She will try to find individuals in the community who can guide Junior thinking in special areas where her own experience may be limited, or where it is wise to supplement what is taking place in the school. For instance, Juniors may at first have little idea as to what it means to be followers of Jesus: merely talking about this may not provide half so enriching an experience as inviting some truly Christian adults who have the respect of the Juniors and who are trying to live by principles of Jesus; and these need not be professional Christian workers.

A school that encourages Juniors to think and to search for answers to their questions is going to make use of the Juniors' own imagination and ability. It will not discount dreaming about ideals and heroic deeds, but it will not be satisfied with dreams alone. A good school will seek to lead the child from such dreaming to prayer and to planning and doing on his own level; it will never try to cut down adult ways of thinking and acting to fit the Junior, but will help the Juniors to live as Christians on their own level, careful always to recognize that there must be growth, and that all wholesome growth is slow growth. So the teacher will not think in terms of separate lessons, though this course will offer plans for a specific number of lessons; she will see that an ongoing experience in Christian living and thinking is taking place and that the boys and girls are responsible with her for planning and carrying on such experiences. A practical suggestion is that every teacher jot down important learning experiences in her group, and Junior points of view as these are revealed in discussion and planning periods; these notes will provide a certain continuity in the school and a basis for gathering evidences of individual growth. The Juniors will need facts, stories, even drill in the mechanics of the Bible, but, after all, the important thing from a Christian point of view is what is done with these — how they change life and help in the growth of Christian character.

So a teacher has many things to think about as she prepares to teach. She must decide for herself, as she thinks about her purpose, what are the real child needs to which this course will con-

GENERAL PLANS FOR THE DEPARTMENT

tribute. She will need to think about the significant facts that boys and girls must know, what questions will stimulate their thinking, what materials will be needed to help them to find the answers to some of their questions; she will need to think about interesting activities which will provide rich experiences in living and working together as Christians for the duration of the school. (Suggestions for such activities will be found on page 193.) She will be ever alert to see that plans for worship provide something vital and beautiful for Junior worshipers; she will never forget that this will come about best as worship grows out of living experience.

A MINIMUM LIST OF WORK MATERIALS [1]

Cartons and boxes of various sorts and sizes for construction work
Chalk
Cloth — small squares — for cleaning, dusting, and so forth
Crayolas, 3 or 4 boxes for each group working in color
Eraser, 1 to a group (unless pencils have them)
Orange crates for making bookcases and other furniture if this is needed by the Juniors
Paper: 2 packages 9" x 12" gray or brown bogus, for construction work and bookmaking
1 package 9" x 12" assorted colored sheets construction paper, for book covers, posters, and so forth
Large, smooth sheets of wrapping paper
Paste, 1 jar to each assistant and her group
Pencils, 1 for each Junior
Scissors, 2 or 3 to a group
Thumbtacks

ADDITIONAL WORK MATERIALS [1]

Boards — three-ply soft pine boards cut in 3' lengths or the smooth sides of thin wooden boxes — for making cutouts

[1] With the exception of glass slides, pine boards, and such materials as can be brought from home, all these items can be obtained from your own denominational bookstores, from Milton Bradley Company, or from any house selling supplies for school or Church School.

Coping saws and blades for making cutouts
Cardboard — thin sheets — for book covers or construction
Craft paper for construction according to need
Crayon chalks in color for construction or blackboard work
Glass slides for making lantern slides (see Keystone catalogue)
Onion-skin parchment sheets, caked camphor, and alcohol, for making stained-glass window effects
Jars, muffin tins, and so forth, for mixing paint and washing brushes
Paintbrushes, medium size
Poster paints
Patterns — cutouts of animals or dolls — Milton Bradley Company (see catalogue)
Pencils — colored — for work on slides and so forth
Plasteline, tagboard, or clothespins for figure-making in miniature scenes
Sewing materials for dressing dolls

SUGGESTIONS FOR ACTIVE GAMES [1]

"Japanese Tag." As in all tag games, "It" pursues the rest of the players and tries to touch one of them. When one has been touched, he must keep his hand on the spot where he was touched and pursue the others. His hand cannot be freed from this spot until he has tagged someone else. The idea is to tag people in inconvenient places, on the ankle, on the knee, et cetera.

"Object-passing Tag." The group selects some object, which is passed by handing it from one to the other. This may be a ball, handkerchief, or stone. One can be tagged only when he has this object in his possession. Another player must take it as soon as it is offered to him; if he refuses to do so, he immediately becomes "It."

"Goal." Arrange the players in a circle and have them stand with their legs wide apart. Secure a large ball for this game, such as a football or basketball. One player stands in the center

---

[1] Quoted from *The Cokesbury Game Book*, by Arthur M. Depew. Used by permission of the Abingdon-Cokesbury Press, publishers.

GENERAL PLANS FOR THE DEPARTMENT 179

with a ball and tries to score a goal by rolling the ball between the outstretched legs of some player in the circle. Those who are in the circle may defend the "goal" only by using their hands to prevent the ball's passing between their legs and must not at any time of the game bring their legs together. Unless the ball is coming toward a player, he should have his hands on his hips. When the player in the center scores a goal, the player on whom the score is made must take his place in the center and must stay there until he succeeds in scoring.

"**Rabbit.**" The players are divided into groups of three and are scattered into groups around the playground. Two of the three form a "home," facing each other and joining hands. The third one will be the "rabbit" and will simply stand in this house.

In addition to these groups of three, there should be two extra players, a homeless rabbit and a hunter. The hunter starts the game by chasing the homeless rabbit around and around, in and out the groups. When the rabbit has grown tired, he may go into one of the homes, and at once the rabbit who was already there must leave, and this rabbit is chased by the hunter. When the hunter catches a rabbit, the two change places, the hunter becoming the rabbit, and the rabbit becoming the hunter.

"**Crows and Cranes.**" "Crows and Cranes" is a game which is entirely active but will provide lots of entertainment for a group of young people. There is no equipment required except a coin and a leader for the game.

Following are the directions for the leader:

Divide the group into two equal sides. Name one of the teams "Crows" and the other team "Cranes." Line the two teams up four or five feet apart, facing each other. Flip the coin, and if it lands heads up, call "Crows." Upon the calling of "Crows," the "Crows" must turn in flight, with the "Cranes" after them. If any of the "Cranes" succeeds in touching a member (or members) of the "Crows" before he crosses a given line (this line may be from twenty to sixty feet behind the original line), he is considered a captive of the "Cranes" and must aid the "Cranes" when play is continued. If the coin should land tails up, the "Cranes" must turn in flight, with the "Crows" chasing them and endeavoring to capture the "Cranes." Continue flipping the coin, each time calling "Crows" or "Cranes." The team succeeding in capturing all members of the other team is declared the winner.

SUGGESTED BOOKS AND MATERIALS FOR WORKERS AND JUNIORS

Few schools can buy all the books and materials they would like to, yet many schools appreciate suggestions of various types of books and supplies from which choices can be made. Often books can be borrowed from ministers and other interested friends of the school. With the exception of Bibles and hymnbooks and perhaps a few pictures, none of the following books are absolutely essential to the success of the school; this course provides all basic materials. In "A Minimum List of Work Materials," on page 177, there is a minimum list suggested for those leaders who have a small fund to spend on new books, and who want to know which would be most directly useful in the work of the school. The classified lists which follow are offered for the stimulation of teachers who wish to do some reading in the field of teaching method, or who have little in the way of additional story and working materials and who wish to discover what is readily available.

BOOKS OF GENERAL METHOD

(For the use of teachers of experience who want to know more of the purposes and methods of the Activity Program.)

Finding Wisdom, by Gertrude Hartman. The John Day Company. For the splendid portrayal of children working by activity methods, and for the illustration in color of children at work and examples of their finished work. Price, $3.00.

A Teacher's Guide Book to the Activity Program, by Robert Hill Lane. The Macmillan Company. A clear, concise statement of the principles and procedures involved. Price, $2.00.

The Activity Program, by A. Gordon Melvin. The John Day

Company. Giving a detailed picture of how the activity program works out in school situations. Price, $3.50.

Activities in the Public School, by Margaret Gustin and Margaret L. Hayes. The University of North Carolina Press. Carries illustrations of children at work, and concrete illustrations of how an activity gets under way. Teachers would need to adapt the method to activities which grow more naturally out of the Church School situation, but the method of work is identical. Price, $2.00.

SPECIFIC METHOD ADAPTED FOR USE IN THE VACATION CHURCH SCHOOL

The New Vacation Church School, by W. Dyer Blair. Harper & Brothers. Without being in any sense a course, the book offers suggestions on the organization, administration, and equipment of the Vacation Church School. The book explains how to utilize the creative experience of children in discussion, worship, music, drama, handwork, and play. Price, $1.50.

Teaching Junior Boys and Girls, by Mildred Moody Eakin. Abingdon-Cokesbury Press. Gives guidance to new teachers who are anxious to learn the best approach to boys and girls, and specific procedures which will make for the happiest working conditions in the school. Price, $1.25.

BOOKS USEFUL TO BOTH LEADERS AND JUNIORS FOR BOTH UNITS

Biblical Materials and Hymnals.
For Units I and II — A large Bible with good print.

I and II — Individual Bibles for the Juniors to use in study (wherever possible, Juniors should be encouraged to bring their own).

I and II — One of the later translations of the Bible, such as that of James Moffatt.

I — A one-volume Bible dictionary, such as that of James Hastings.

I — A Bible concordance for Junior use.

I and II — *The Junior Bible,* edited by Edgar J. Goodspeed.

The Macmillan Company. In the Bible text, with readable type and excellent line drawings. To be used with guidance with older Juniors. Price, $2.50.

I and II — *The Children's Bible,* translated and arranged by Henry A. Sherman and Charles Foster Kent. Charles Scribner's Sons. For use with younger Juniors, especially the stories of Jesus and of his disciples. Price, $1.00 and $2.50.

I and II — *The Secret,* by Harold Burdekin. E. P. Dutton & Co., Inc. Contains full-page photos illustrating the Biblical principle of love at work in everyday life. Some of the pictures are better for mature picture lovers, but many of them will prove delightful and valuable to Juniors who use the book under guidance. Price, $1.75.

I — *The Greatest Name,* by Elsie Ball. Abingdon-Cokesbury Press. This book will give Junior readers a better understanding as to why Jesus' friends felt about him as they did. Price, $1.50.

II — *The Story of Our Bible,* by Harold B. Hunting. Charles Scribner's Sons. Especially Chapters 39–45, dealing with the translation of the Bible into many languages. Price, $2.50.

II — *The World in Which Jesus Lived,* by Basil Mathews. Abingdon-Cokesbury Press. Especially Chapters 7 and 8, dealing with Paul's adventures. Price, $1.50.

I and II — Your own denominational hymnal and the hymnal used by the Juniors.

Collections of Stories for Reading Table or for Telling.
For Units I and II — *The Children's Story Caravan,* edited by Anna P. Broomell. J. B. Lippincott Company. Price, $2.00.

II — *Missionary Stories to Tell,* compiled by the Children's Committee of the Missionary Education Movement. Friendship Press. Price: cloth, $1.00; paper, 50 cents.

II — *Far Round the World,* by Grace W. McGavran. Friendship Press. Stories of missionaries and others who follow the Christ. Price: cloth, $1.00; paper, 50 cents.

II — *The Friendly Missionary,* by Nina Millen. Friendship Press. Though planned for Primary readers, this little book gives much background concerning ways in which missionaries help today which younger Juniors will enjoy. Price, 25 cents.

PICTURES

Books Containing Pictures.
For Unit II — *The Life of Jesus,* selected and arranged by Myrtle K. Wilde. W. A. Wilde Company. Jesus' life as pictured by the master painters of the world. Parts I and II, 25 cents each.

II — *Each with His Own Brush,* by Daniel Johnson Fleming. Friendship Press. Dealing with contemporary Christian art in mission lands of Asia and Africa, and containing 65 splendid reproductions of paintings and carvings of the Christ. Price, $1.50.

Pictures. Pictures of Jesus and of his disciples clipped and mounted for study and enjoyment by the Juniors. They may be annotated on the back by the Juniors if desired. Beginners and Primary Superintendents often keep files of such pictures selected from the Sunday School picture sets and are glad to lend them.

Selected pictures of modern Christians at work especially in everyday situations, children as well as adults, should be included among the pictures.

The following list of pictures has been selected from the Perry Pictures catalogue, which can be obtained for 15 cents by writing the company at Malden, Massachusetts. The list is one which suggests paintings from all ages of Christian art and by all types of artists. Two primitives have been included (those of Giotto and Gaddi) as examples of the simple, childlike art of the first artists; they brought a depth of love rather than of technical ability to the job of painting. Juniors can be helped to appreciate these, because the pictures of Giotto and Gaddi are among the very first of the age when men were free to paint Christ, not according to rule, but according to the way they felt about him. In ordering please note that no orders for less than fifty cents will be accepted by The Perry Pictures Company.

The five pictures in the first group are in 10" x 12" size done in sepia; price, 10 cents each. They can also be obtained in the 2-cent group:

321. *Sistine Madonna,* by **Raphael.**
801. *Head of Christ,* by **Hofmann.**
807. *Christ Blessing Little Children,* by **Plockhörst.**
831. *Christ Before Pilate,* by **Munkácsy.**
1101. *Christ and the Fishermen,* by **Zimmermann.**

The fifteen pictures in the second group are in 5½" x 8" size, at 2 cents each; those marked with asterisk (*) may also be secured in 3" x 3½" size at 1 cent each; the few marked 10 cents are also available at that price in 10" x 12" size finished in sepia. The first nine pictures listed are planned specifically for use with Unit II. The list will need to be augmented by an additional ten pictures, ordered in addition to the selections above, in order to meet the minimum order requirement:

204*. *Madonna,* by Giotto.
212. *Adoration of the Magi,* by Taddeo Gaddi.
222–O. *Madonna della Stella,* by Fra Angelico.
222–P. *The Annunciation and Adoration of the Magi,* by Fra Angelico.
280*. *The Last Supper,* by Da Vinci (10 cents).
299*. *Holy Family,* by Michelangelo.
324*. *Madonna of the Chair,* by Raphael (10 cents).
343–N*. *St. Paul,* by Raphael.
360*. *John the Baptist,* by Del Sarto (10 cents).
797–I*. *Sermon on the Mount,* by Hofmann.
797–S*. *Christ in the Home of Mary and Martha,* by Hofmann.
798–B*. *On the Way to Emmaus,* by Hofmann.
1268*. *The Christ,* by Thorwaldsen.
3302*. "*Come Unto Me, All Ye That Labor,*" by Bloch.
3235*. *Light of the World,* by Holman Hunt (10 cents).

FOR USE WITH STEREOPTICON MACHINES

No list of slides is carried here because there are so many possibilities to choose from. Write to any of the following companies, asking for catalogues and price lists, and make your own selections, keeping in mind the need to present only the pictures most suitable for Juniors in the light of your purpose in showing them:

Kansas City Slide Company, 1719 Wyandotte Street, Kansas City, Missouri.

National Pictures Service, Inc., 324 East 3d Street, Cincinnati, Ohio.

Riley and Riley, 21 Stephens Place, Staten Island, New York.

Victor Animatograph Corporation, Davenport, Iowa.

GENERAL PLANS FOR THE DEPARTMENT

Williams, Brown & Earle, Inc., 918 Chestnut Street, Philadelphia, Pennsylvania.

Denominational publishing houses and mission boards.

FOR USE WITH A FILM-STRIP PROJECTOR

Most film strips are sold rather than rented. Lists of available subjects can be secured from the Society for Visual Education, 100 East Ohio Street, Chicago, Illinois. The following are typical of what this company offers:

3. *Miracles and Public Life of Christ*, 38 frames ($2.00).

52B. *The Calling of Disciples to the Rejection of Nazareth*, 30 frames ($2.00).

68B. *The Story of Peter and the Early Church*, 30 frames ($2.00).

70B. *The Early Church, The Story of Paul*, Parts I and II, 30 frames (price per part, $2.00).

71B. *The Early Church, The Story of Paul*, Parts I and II, 30 frames (price per part, $2.00).

The Westminster Press offers the following film strips for $2.00 a set in black and white. Prices in color will be quoted on request. Teacher's Manual accompanies each strip.

The Life of Christ, by Harold Copping, 36 frames. Frames 8–24 present the life and work of Christ from call of the disciples to the entry into Jerusalem. Price, $2.00.

The Life of Paul (the first 15 frames) and *The Parables of Jesus* on one strip, by Harold Copping, 27 frames. Price, $2.00.

SUGGESTIONS FOR PUPIL ACTIVITIES

Some teachers think of pupil activities chiefly in terms of "making things." Anything that engages pupil attention and stimulates a pupil mentally or bodily provides genuine activity. Contributing thoughtfully to a group discussion is as truly pupil activity as is making toy cutouts for a children's hospital. The activity chosen by pupils depends upon their purpose; no activity which is not a means of carrying out worth-while purpose has a place in a Vacation Church School.

Certain activities are written into the session plans in detail, and so do not appear on the list below. The list given here offers suggestions as to types of additional activity which serve Juniors as they develop purposes of their own. Many of the suggestions can be substituted for or added to the special activities which appear in the session plans. It is important to keep in mind that no craftwork or other activity should ever be added to the work of the Vacation School as an additional attraction; it must be obvious to pupil and leader alike that any activity under way is necessary for the successful carrying out of pupil plans and purposes.

DRAWING AND PAINTING

Making posters which tell the story of some of Jesus' followers or ways in which various persons or groups have followed him through the ages. These posters may be planned as group activities in which a whole series is worked out in co-operation, and single incidents in the series may be assigned to one or more Juniors to complete. The finished work of the group will have value only as each working member does his best thinking and work. An adaptation of this plan is the making of a frieze, the various sections of which can be assigned in much the same way as the individual posters were, after group planning is complete. Posters or frieze may be done either as crayon drawings or in poster paints.

Making designs for book covers and illustrations for a record of discoveries or similar pupil-made book. " Peak " points or incidents or stories will be chosen for illustration according to their appeal or value to the Juniors who do the planning and illustrating. Designs for book covers may carry some motif from the book content which will emphasize its theme or its special appeal. For example, a simple fishing boat or stretches of drying nets could be worked into effective designs for a book of stories concerning Jesus choosing his first helpers.

Making slides which tell the story of Jesus' followers long ago or today. This will make an especially fine activity in those schools which own or can borrow a projector which takes the standard-size slide of $3\frac{1}{4}''$ x $4''$ (see list of work materials on page 178). In one school where such slides were made and displayed by a group studying the life of Christ, a Junior interpreted the meaning of each picture and its background as it was thrown on the screen. An interesting set could be made on the many ways in which a missionary helps as a follower of Jesus, or the ways Juniors can find of being followers. Pupils may draw and color their pictures on etched glass of the proper size. Full particulars and methods of making handmade slides may be secured free from The Keystone View Company, Meadville, Pennsylvania.

Making a stained-glass window (Juniors to plan) which will help worshipers to understand and think about what it means to be a follower of Jesus. Transparent paper having a parchment-like finish will be best for this. To prepare the paper (which should be one made of linen or cotton rags), put it to soak for about an hour in an alcohol bath in which has been dissolved as much camphor as the alcohol will take. A tiny bit of dye of any desired color may also be added to the alcohol. Spread the paper out smoothly and let it dry. It will take dye or color readily after this treatment, and the Juniors can add their own design or pictures in color, and place the finished drawing in place over the window, fastening it securely with a touch of paste at the outer edges. If a full-size window is to be made, the paper may be designed in sections, making sure that careful markings are in place on the edge of each sheet if the design or picture is to be continued from one sheet to another. Or, the window can be made in sections, each section carrying its own design or small picture. If this activity should be chosen, the Juniors may wish to take a trip to visit some church having stained-glass windows. Before they begin their work they will want to think about reasons for having such decoration in a church, and what they want their window, when finished, to say to worshipers.

Painting Backgrounds for Miniature Scenes (see under "Craftwork and Special Activities"). Except that the painting will be done on small sheets of paper at the table, the work of planning and executing the backgrounds will be similar to working on scenery for a large play (see following). Water colors or poster paints can be used with brushes.

Drawing and Painting Scenery for a Play. In the informal dramatization of stories, scenery is not actually necessary. However, if a group of Juniors are planning to give a play and want to carry through all the steps involved, including the making of costumes and scenery as well as the writing and rehearsing of parts, there are good reasons why they should be allowed to do so. The first step is finding out what the scenery should portray (see "Dramatizing a Story," which follows). Looking at pictures to discover the kinds of trees and flowers common to the scene in which the action is to take place, or what the buildings, market place, or street scene would be like in the story is a first important step. When the Juniors have decided what the background is to be, and how it will contribute to the story, they may wish to sketch the background roughly on small papers. When the content and arrangement have been thus determined, large sheets of wrapping paper may be fastened on the wall which is to be used as the backdrop, and each Junior painter should understand clearly which is his section to paint, and exactly what part of the completed drop he is to make. Boxes or even stepladders can be used to help the painters to complete the whole of their panels or sections, or the sheets can be laid on the floor and painted there, being put into place afterward. The children who can draw best may sketch in the trees, buildings, or figures and the others may color them. When completed, the sections of scenery can be thumbtacked into place or tacked into thin wooden frames which can be stood against the wall. Fine detailed work should be discouraged, as large, sweeping strokes will give the best color effects. The color can be put on as finger painting is done. Prepare the color for this by boiling thick starch to which a little glue has been added. Divide up the mixture according to the color needs, adding powdered paints directly to it. Let the Juniors work in the colors with fingers and hands. A little practice gives truly lovely effects. A hot iron run over the back of these panels will fix the color permanently if the Juniors decide that the finished scenery is worthy of being given to the church for other dramatic presentations on special occasions.

DRAMATIZING A STORY

Planning to give a play is not easy, but any group of wide-awake Juniors can have a good time in working one out. First, the story to be dramatized must be chosen. It must not require more characters than can be managed, nor should there be so few characters that only a small number of those who wish to take part can do so.

Setting. When the story has been chosen, the next step is to "make the play." The Juniors must find out what has been done and said in the story; they must discover where the events of the story took place. Was it outside the city? in a house? down by the river? When this has been learned, the Juniors must select locations on the stage or in the front of the room to represent the various locations. Where will the city wall stand? Where does the road come in? Where will the entrance to the house be? The group must also decide where the finished play will be given. Is there a stage? Are there entrances? Can the play be given out of doors?

Scenes. An important part of playmaking is deciding how many scenes are necessary. One, two, or three scenes are usually best. For example, the story of Paul's becoming a follower may be played in two scenes. One scene takes place on the road to Damascus; the other might be played in the house where Paul was blind and alone until Ananias came.

Speech and Action. Planning the speeches and action for each actor is a most important part of the activity. The exact speeches used in the story should be familiar, though it is not necessary for the Juniors to use these in their play. Perhaps the story does not give enough spoken words to tell the whole story. The Juniors would have to imagine what was said by the soldiers when they saw Paul fall and fill in what Paul said to them when he discovered that he was blind. Much of this can be done in actual rehearsal. The story will be studied for action as well as spoken words, for the actors must not only let the audience see what they are doing but often explain in words how they came to do it. Each scene must be worked out so carefully that the audience will be able to follow the story.

Rehearsals. The next step may be rehearsing the play. Every Junior wishing to take part should have a chance to try out for a part. Every actor must understand that he is trying out and may not be chosen after all if someone does that particular part better than he. After all, "the play's the thing," and the group will want to take pride in seeing that it is well done. Also, there is much need for sceneshifters, curtain tender, property and costume makers, and other helpers, as well as for actors, and these are as necessary to the success of the play as the actors. Each Junior who is trying out for a part will do the best he can, and be willing to accept criticism; he must even be willing to see someone else chosen for the part if the group feels that another does it better. The Juniors can be helped to see that they are not giving the play just for their own enjoyment, but to share it with others, and that willingness to take a lesser place is a real part of being a good follower.

During the tryout when an actor hesitates, not knowing what to do next, he may be helped by the others in the watching group who may suggest words and action appropriate to the event being played. Such filling in must be done in the light of the story's purpose and content. Sometimes the best help a critic can offer a hesitating actor is to suggest that he look in the Bible again to see if the story hints at what might be said or done next.

When all who wish to do so have tried out in one or more parts, the entire group should decide on the final cast in the light of the tryouts. The story should be played many times in an informal way, with no learned parts, before the final choices for the cast are made. Suggestions for improving speeches and actions may be given.

It is not at all necessary to write the play, though some of the actors may wish to write out an important line or two of a speech if it has been decided to use the actual words spoken in the original story at some point in the play. For the most part, all that is necessary is that the players shall be perfectly familiar with the story events and purpose and that their impromptu words shall be in keeping with the story action. Actual parts need not be memorized. Juniors should discover that the best of all plays for them is one in which the actors know the story so well that they can make up their speeches and actions as they go along. Plans for scenes, assignments of responsibility for making costumes, scenery, and properties, if these are to be used, and other important matters should be recorded in some way, perhaps on the blackboard.

Costumes and Properties. Most stories can be given with

few or no costumes or properties. All of them can be given with fairly simple arrangements. A dark screen, for example, does very well for a wall or an interior, although some Junior groups will want to draw and paint their own backgrounds on large sheets of light-colored wrapping paper. In dramatizing Bible stories, a couch cover and a Turkish towel make a very satisfactory costume if they are draped as shown here in the picture. A bright-colored cord or band to go around the " turban " can be secured from almost any scrap bag. For more elaborate costumes, pieces of cloth and Turkish toweling from the five-and-ten can be dyed at home or in the church kitchen, pressed, and cut out according to the simple pattern given here. Fold the material in half twice. Then place the material so that there is a fold at the top and a fold at the right side. Then cut as shown by the heavy lines on the pattern. The small piece for the neck should be cut out only in front. An overdrape of contrasting color should be used. Two important points in making plans are: (1) to plan no more than can be done by the group in the time allowed; (2) to stick to the plan when it is once undertaken and see it through in good Junior fashion.

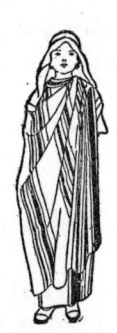

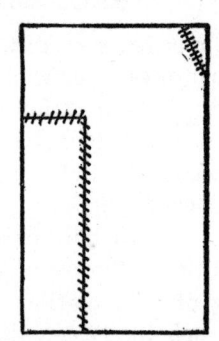

CREATIVE WRITING

Printing of newspaper items (either by hand or with a printing set) for the bulletin board, announcing the completion of Giotto's picture of Christ, of the Bible printed in English, of Luther's and Livingstone's adventures, and other news events " reported " in the second unit.

Writing a book of Bible stories of characters studied, to be read to Primary children who cannot yet read easily.

Making a history book (illustrated), telling what Jesus' followers have done in the world, beginning with the work of the disciples. (A special activity for older Juniors.)

FACT-GATHERING

Making plans for a reading corner and for the safekeeping of books, magazines, poems, and pictures which can help us to gather interesting information for our use in this course. Using the reading corner constructively and co-operatively.

Visiting a beautiful church, or studying our own church interior to get ideas for making a " stained-glass " window or slides, or to see how church buildings use beauty to remind us of the meaning of being followers of Jesus.

Gathering of information about modern everyday followers of Jesus through interviews with people, through outside reading, through actual discovery of new or overlooked reminders of followers of Jesus; such things as tablets, memorial windows, and so forth, monuments to bravery and unselfish service (not in connection with war) for others.

Visiting an art gallery to look at masterpieces of art whose painters or sculptors have thus told us something of Christ.

Visiting some community institution where followers of Jesus are actually at work for others. Such institutions as day nurseries, visiting nurse associations, the office of a hospital (probably the children would not be permitted in the wards), or the office of a city missionary employed by some church where Christian service is actually being carried out will open the eyes of many Juniors who have not understood what is really happening in these fields. Such visitations should be planned in advance, so that workers will be ready to answer questions and make explanations. Plans for co-operating in some way with some of these institutions ought to be an outcome of such a visit. Suggestions for gifts to be made for such places are given below.

CRAFTWORK AND SPECIAL ACTIVITIES

Making Jigsaw Toys. This activity could probably best be carried out by older Juniors who are interested in preparing gifts for distribution to some hospital children's ward, day nursery, or the like. The Milton Bradley Company, Springfield, Massachusetts, and other houses carry patterns for jointed animals and fairy-tale characters. Paper-doll patterns can be obtained easily, and arms and legs made separately. These patterns should be traced on three-ply soft pine boards, and cut out with a jig saw. The edges should be sandpapered smoothly, and the toys painted when finished. Eyes and mouth and perhaps the hairline or fur may need to be drawn before painting in. Arms and legs may be nailed in place with small, slender brads, and the nail ends cut closely with a wire cutter. Of course, there is no reason why the Juniors should not make their own patterns, thus adding much to the interest and originality of the work.

Dressing Dolls. As an outcome of interest in some particular institutional work for children, older girls might be interested in dressing small, inexpensive dolls for distribution to the children concerned or as a gift to some mission school or other station where children's work is carried on.

Making Book Covers. Attractive book covers can be made in various ways. Here is an interesting way to decorate book covers which have been cut from thin cardboard in correct size to fit the book pages: On slightly larger sheets of brown paper make overlays of color with pastel chalk which give effects of mottled color (the way tiny children scribble color over all without line or design). When the paper is well covered with pleasing effects of color (reds and blues, or browns and greens and orange make very satisfying combinations) crumble and lightly rub the paper through between the hands until the whole is soft and pliable, and the colors have been shaded together. Paste a soft padding over the cardboard covers (thin sheets of cotton wadding are ideal, but folded scraps of cloth cut to fit will do very well) and press under weight. When this is perfectly dry lay the padded side down on the exact center upon the wrong side of the colored crushed paper cover which has been prepared, and draw lightly around this with a pencil. Lift the cardboard and trim the paper cover so that it is just large enough to make about a half inch fold all around. Then miter the corners and fold over the cardboard, trimming the corners neatly. Paste the cardboard edge over which this half-inch flap will be folded, and press the cover over it to fit. The cover should be stretched smoothly and evenly in place as the whole lies flat on a table, before it is finally allowed to adhere in place. Cut a paper lining about $\frac{1}{8}$ inch smaller than the cardboard, and paste one side of it smoothly. Lay down on the wrong side of the book cover so that the folded flap is covered evenly on all sides. Press the whole under a weight, and complete the back book cover in the same way. Fold a piece of cardboard two inches wider than is needed to hold the thickness of the book pages, and in which to insert the left edge of the book pages. Prepare a brown paper cover exactly as you did for the other two pieces of cardboard, except that the paper should be cut to fit, and not lapped over the edges, and no cloth lining is necessary. Paste in place and dry under weight, first making sure that the creases have not been lost with the adding of the brown paper. When all is dry cut out letters by hand or clip matched capital letters from a magazine in which to spell out the title of the book. Paste these in place (they need not be in straight line; sometimes a slanting line is much more attractive) and shellac over both covers and back edge piece with plain, thin, white shellac. If any drawn design is to be added for cover decoration this should be done before the chalk color is added and the paper crumbled. The whole makes a very durable and most attractive cover, which can be punched and laced or sewed with colored ribbon or cord.

Such covers might be planned for Bible storybooks, as gifts for younger children, or for other gift-making. One group of girls saved recipes from the daily paper and made recipe books for their mothers, while the boys saved crossword puzzles and the correct answers appearing the next day and made some most attractive gifts for hospital distribution, putting the puzzles in the front part of the book and the correct answers in the back.

Making miniature scenes showing events in the work of the disciples, showing followers in the Early Church, or perhaps showing some missionary or other modern follower of Jesus at work. These scenes can be made in boxes which have been placed on their sides. The appropriate backgrounds, including such things as mountains, roads, buildings, or sky, may be painted on paper to fit and then pasted on the bottom and sides of the box. Figures of people can be cut from paper and painted, or modeled of plasteline. A paper figure will stand if the bottom of the figure is extended and folded, then pasted to the floor of the scene. Standing figures can be represented by dressed clothespins, which will stand erect if thrust into corrugated cardboard and can be added as needed to represent the action. Other small properties which may be needed can be molded, or cut from paper and held in place by paste. The front of the box through which the scene is viewed may be covered with cellophane if desired. Cartons about a foot deep and two or three feet long are most usable. Remove the front and top sides of the box before going to work.

Making a vivarium for the safekeeping of toads, lizards, turtles, or other living creatures which may be brought to school by Juniors, who often like such pets. Instead of discouraging the bringing in of such creatures, it is far better to encourage Juniors to care for them properly and to feel responsible for their well-being. Juniors should be helped to see the need for discovering whether their pets require dry or wet quarters. Granite pans or shallow glass bowls (preferably not too small or round) make a good foundation. Tin or other metal unprotected by enamel should not be used. Moss placed over gravel makes a good home for any of the creatures listed above. Tiny plants embedded in the moss will grow nicely if kept wet. Pebble paths, a mirror lake made of a smooth-edged pocket mirror, tiny bridges or figures bought at the five-and-ten, or modeled in clay and baked in the sun or home oven, will add much to the looks of such a place. Of course, the whole should be kept very damp. A tiny, shallow dish, perhaps a bird's treat cup, half-buried in the moss, will provide drinking water. Food will depend on the specific needs of the creatures; usually small bugs or flies are usable, or bits of ground meat. Tadpoles, minnows, or other water creatures, of course, would need an out-and-out tank or glass bowl of water free of contact with unsurfaced metal, a pebbly bottom, and water plants taken from a near-by stream or bought at a pet store. Such creatures should not be crowded. Usually one or two is all that such temporary homes will care for. In no case should creatures antagonistic to one another be put together, such as lizards and turtles, or toads and fish. Nor should turtles or toads be put in water bowls or aquariums. They need only a general dampness and very shallow stretches of water, not the depth required by fish. Above all, they need dry rocks or stones for resting places in the sun.

Such a vivarium or aquarium will make a very acceptable gift for a sick or shut-in child, particularly if directions for the continued care of the little creature and its home accompany the gift.

PLANNING SPECIAL PROGRAMS AND CARRYING THEM THROUGH

In both of the following possibilities for sharing, the Juniors will need to be guarded against over elaboration.

Planning Special Assembly Programs. Almost anything of real interest is good " stuff " for calling the school together. Now and then some group makes an interesting discovery — it may be a new story or pictures that explain something that the group has been wondering about; or the members of a group may have completed some piece of work which will serve the whole department and wish to explain about the gift and its use and care; or perhaps some problem important enough to call for the thinking of the group as a whole faces the children. Any of these are typical occasions when an assembly may seem wise. Now and then some interesting visitor will be in the neighborhood and may be asked by the children to visit the school and answer questions, tell of his work or a trip he has taken, or demonstrate some way of using tools; this too is a cause for assembling the school as a whole, perhaps without the Beginners Department. In all such cases careful and definite plans for the program as a whole, including someone to meet the speaker and introduce him and someone responsible for each part of the program, should be provided by the children themselves in consultation with their leaders.

Planning for a Final Program and Exhibit. Many schools like to close their term by inviting the parents and friends of the Juniors in to visit the department, see the finished work of the Juniors, listen to their explanations and special presentations of certain phases of their work. If a dramatization has been worked out, this will undoubtedly be a feature. The program should be thought of by the Juniors, not as a "show-off" day, but as an opportunity to share with others some of their happiest experiences in living and learning together. Details for such a program must be made up out of the work of the term and the definite planning of the Juniors, who should assume full responsibility for the program and the exhibits. This entire list of activities offers much by way of suggestion for such a program.